# PIVOT POINT

## PIVOT POINT FUNDAMENTALS: COSMETOLOGY
## LONG HAIR DESIGN

1st Edition
4th Printing, October 2021
Printed in China

Pivot Point International, Inc.
Global Headquarters
8725 West Higgins Road, Suite 700
Chicago, IL 60631 USA

847-866-0500
pivot-point.com

D1293844

# CONTENTS

## 108ᶜ // LONG HAIR DESIGN

Long Hair Theory ........................................ 2

Long Hair Tools and Essentials .................... 17

Long Hair Skills ........................................ 30

Long Hair Guest Experience ...................... 52

Long Hair Service .................................... 68

52

Single-Strand Twists Workshop ........................................... 77

2-Strand Overlap Workshop ................................................ 83

3-Strand Overbraid Workshop ............................................. 90

3-Strand Underbraid Workshop ........................................... 96

On-the-Scalp 3-Strand Braids Workshop ...... 102

Single-Strand, Coiled Twists Workshop ........ 109

5-Strand Loops Workshop ................................................ 118

Vertical Roll Workshop ..................................................... 125

30   52   17

# LONG HAIR
## THEORY
# 108<sup>c</sup>.1 >

## EXPLORE //

**Think of a friend or relative who has had her hair put up for a special occasion. Did her long hair design meet her expectations and hold up to the demands of the event?**

## INSPIRE //

Your ability to analyze form, texture and direction and envision the possibilities you can create will keep you in demand with long hair clients.

## ACHIEVE //

Following this lesson on *Long Hair Theory,* you'll be able to:

>> Explain the levels of observation used to analyze a long hair design

>> Restate in your own words how changing the long hair design can dramatically affect a client's appearance

## FOCUS //

**LONG HAIR THEORY**

Long Hair Design Analysis

Change the Long Hair Design, Change the Effect

## 108ᶜ.1
## LONG HAIR THEORY

Long hair design opportunities include styling for runway shows, editorial photo shoots and servicing bridal clients. Though long hair trends change over time, many of the techniques used to create them remain consistent. With a solid repertoire of long hair techniques and procedures, you can confidently and successfully pursue creative, profitable career opportunities.

Hair designers benefit from learning long hair as a way to expand their clientele. Those especially passionate about long hair see it as a creative art form and even specialize exclusively in long hair design for special occasions, such as weddings.

Successful long hair designing starts with the consultation: when you begin to formulate the design vision, including the form, texture, color and direction of the style. Being able to analyze this vision and having an awareness of how a long hair design changes a client's appearance are crucial in pleasing your long hair clients.

# LONG HAIR DESIGN ANALYSIS

Understanding how to look at a photo using the basic, detail and abstract levels of observation allows you to:

>> Reproduce what you see.

>> Communicate clearly to your client.

>> Begin building your repertoire of ideas and techniques.

>> Adapt and personalize designs for your clients.

## LEVELS OF OBSERVATION
### Basic Level – Form and Shape

>> Outer shape or outline of 3-dimensional form, identified by position of volume

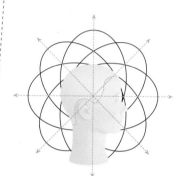  

### Detail Level – Texture and Color

>> Determine type(s) of textures:
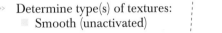 Smooth (unactivated)

 Rough (activated)

>> Determine techniques used to create texture

>> Determine how color affects the design

### Abstract Level – Direction

>> Identify overall direction and directions within form

 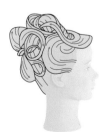 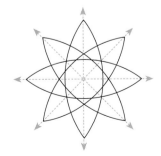

>>>> FORM AND SHAPE

In long hair designing, it is the placement of mass, or volume–not the length arrangement–that creates the overall shape or 3-dimensional form. Volume can be positioned in a specific area or throughout the design.

Long hair designs usually have a **focal point**, which is an area where the eye is drawn and the main emphasis of volume or mass is placed. Keep these points in mind:

>> Placing volume in specific areas visually affects the proportions of the face and neck.

>> Positioning volume can create a flattering overall shape for the client.

>> Altering size of specific element(s) also changes overall proportions of design.

>> Observe your work carefully from different angles to ensure eye-pleasing results, viewed from all directions.

>> Trends and fashions may also apply in placement of volume.

## Equal Height and Width

>> Volume positioned equally throughout long hair design

>> Attention not focused on any particular area

## More Height Than Length

>> Volume positioned in specific area (i.e., crown or nape)

>> Automatically draws the eye to that area

>> Usually draws attention diagonally to crown or vertically to top

## More Length Than Height

>> Focuses attention at nape or below shoulders

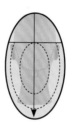

## More Width Than Height or Length

>> Draws the eye horizontally across design

In some instances, fillers (loose fibers or padding) can be used to expand a design or to create specific forms or shapes.

The overall form of a design can be broken down further by analyzing the shape(s) within the design. The size and position of individual shapes influence the feeling of the design.

**DISCOVERMORE**

The positioning of volume will often change as long hair trends and fashions change. Research different periods to see how various fashion trends have influenced the amount or placement of volume in long hair designs. While you're at it, look for inspirations and ideas!

## TEXTURE AND COLOR

### Texture

In long hair design, texture is identified as unactivated (smooth) and activated (patterned), influenced by:

>> Technique(s) used

>> Amount of existing or designed curl texure

It's common to see a combination of textures in a long hair design.

### Color

Color can play an integral role by:

>> Leading your eye through the movements of a design

>> Creating a focal point within a design

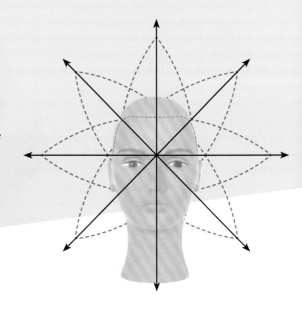

## >>>>>> DIRECTION

The direction of the form is determined by the position of shapes or volume within the design. Lines of the celestial axis can be used to analyze the overall direction as well as the various directions within a long hair design.

>> Clockwise/counterclockwise

>> Vertical/horizontal

>> Diagonal

### Overall Direction
The overall direction of a design may be significantly different when analyzed from various angles.

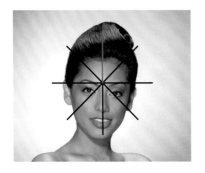

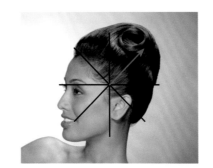

Emphasis at crown:

>> Vertical from front

>> Diagonal from profile view

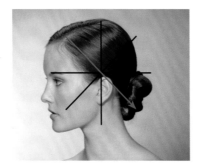

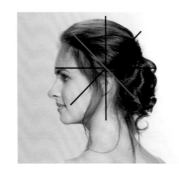

Emphasis at nape:

>> Vertical from behind

>> Diagonal from side

## Directions Within the Design

In long hair designing, hair may:

>> Move in various directions within the design

>> Imply motion

>> Add to dynamics of the design

>> Draw the eye to various focal points or through the design

Observe these examples:

>> Multiple loops

>> Uniform size

>> Various directions

>> Creates interest without overwhelming the eye

>> Fringe area swept upward

>> Clockwise movement

>> Helps to incorporate lengths into remainder of the design

>> Clockwise and counterclockwise knots, loops or curls

>> Positioned along either side

>> Several knots (or curls) positioned closely together at nape

>> Eye is led along lines of distribution to braid

>> Converging along center back

## Proportion and Balance

When planning a well-balanced design, consider the proportional relationship between size, shape, texture and color. The balance can be symmetrical or asymmetrical. The size and position of individual shapes influence the overall feel and impression of the design, allowing you unlimited creative options.

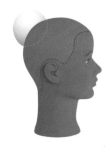

# CHANGE THE LONG HAIR DESIGN, CHANGE THE EFFECT

Long hair design, more than other salon services, requires awareness of the occasion for which the design is created. You and your clients need to agree on the mood or impression to be expressed. During your consultation, gain clarity and agreement on the vision, including the form, texture, color and direction of the design.

Creative options in long hair design are almost infinite, so you can create truly remarkable transformations. To meet and exceed your clients' expectations for every occasion:

» Ask many open-ended questions.

    ▪ What's the occasion?

    ▪ What are you going to wear?

» Listen carefully to your client's answers.

» Confirm understanding.

» Then, make the most effective design decisions for your clients.

A draped braid keeps the front close to the head, emphasizing volume in the back.

Height, volume and texture near the face offset an asymmetric roll creating a diagonally balanced line for a dynamic feeling.

Your success in long hair designing is built on your ability to envision long hair designs and create flattering volume and directional emphasis.

Soft curls move toward the back for an almost romantic feeling.

Unusual, asymmetric placement of volume and an intentionally rougher texture make a contemporary statement.

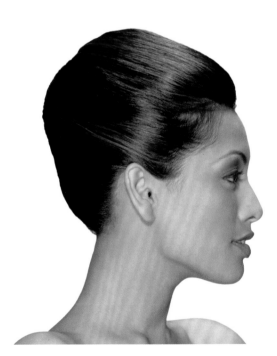

Smooth texture and volume at the crown create a classic, elegant look.

Waves, curls and volume throughout the interior project an unstructured but feminine image.

## SALON**CONNECTION**

**Staying on Top**

Successful designers keep up on the latest long hair trends and techniques so that they can offer clients fresh, new ideas. From red carpets, to proms to weddings—staying on top of what is modern and new keeps stylists relevant and in demand!

## LESSONS LEARNED <<<<<<<

The basic, abstract and detail levels of observation that are used to analyze long hair designs include:

>> Form and shape

>> Texture and color

>> Direction (overall and within the design)

Changing the long hair design can dramatically affect a client's appearance, from romantic to contemporary to classic. The design vision, established during the consultation, includes the form, texture, color and direction of the long hair design.

# 108<sup>c</sup>.2 //
# LONG HAIR TOOLS AND ESSENTIALS

## EXPLORE //

**Do you think you might invest in some tools or products specifically for long hair design? Why?**

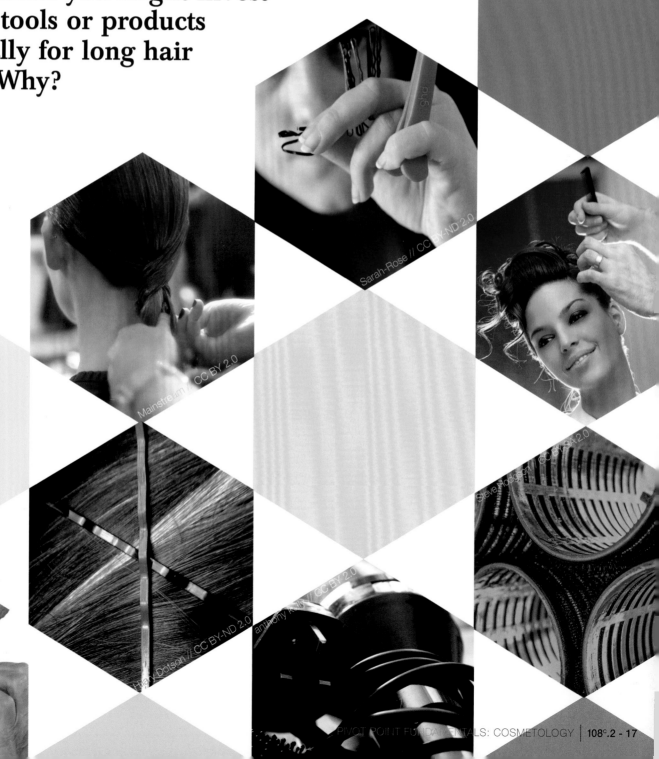

## INSPIRE //

To create a variety of long hair designs, you will choose the tools, supplies and products that best suit each design and client.

## ACHIEVE //

Following this lesson on *Long Hair Tools and Essentials,* you'll be able to:

>> Identify a variety of tools used in long hair design and describe their functions

>> Give examples of supplies commonly used in long hair design and their uses

>> Provide examples of products and equipment used in long hair design and describe their uses

## FOCUS //

### LONG HAIR TOOLS AND ESSENTIALS

| | |
|---|---|
| Thermal Tools | Combs |
| Brushes | Long Hair Essentials |

Designers use many tools, supplies and products to prepare hair for long hair designs. You're already familiar with some of these from your studies in wet and thermal design techniques.

Common tools, supplies and products designers use for hair preparation and during the design include:

>> Blow dryers

>> Air forming brushes

>> Round brushes

>> Thermal rollers

>> Cushion brushes

>> Elastic hair bands

>> Long and short bobby pins and hairpins

>> Synthetic hair fibers

>> Hairnets

Hair designers who are familiar with a variety of tools can offer broader style possibilities to their clients. Using the right tools, supplies and products will help you meet your client's needs based on her hair, desired look and the occasion.

# THERMAL TOOLS

Thermal tools use heat to set desired texture into the hair. Thermal tools used in long hair design are the same as in hair design. The application is adapted to longer lengths and focuses on preparing the hair before putting it up.

## BLOW DRYERS / ATTACHMENTS

Blow dryers and their attachments are used to air form wet hair while using brushes, combs and your fingers to create temporary direction and texture changes.

>> Concentrators, also known as nozzles, focus airflow into a small area.

>> Diffusers spread a gentle airflow over larger areas for wavy or curly textures.

Careful and well-planned drying can make it easier and quicker to put hair up in the finished style.

## THERMAL IRONS

### Curling Irons

>> Temporary curl texture

>> Electric cord, electric base or electric stove

>> Variety of diameters

Professional curling irons are also referred to as marcel irons.

### Flat Irons

>> Temporarily straighten and silk hair

>> Consist of two flat plates

>> Hair is positioned between heated plates to straighten or set texture patterns

## THERMAL ROLLERS

Thermal rollers, or hot rollers, are used on dry hair to quickly add volume and soft texture.

Follow disinfection guidelines provided by your regulatory agency.

# BRUSHES

## AIR FORMING BRUSHES

Brushes, such as vent and 9-row air forming brushes, allow the greatest airflow to the hair so that the lengths can be dried quickly while directing them into the lines of the design.

### 7- or 9-Row

Smooth Finish

### Vent

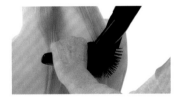

More Movement and Texture

### Paddle

Smooth Finish

## CUSHION BRUSHES

Cushion brushes have dense bristles that can be made of natural fiber, synthetic fiber or a combination. Designers may use this brush on dry hair to:

>> Relax a set

>> Backbrush

>> Increase shine

>> Smooth surface of hair

## ROUND BRUSHES

Round brushes are used to create volume and curved end texture.

They vary in:

>> Diameter

>> Type of bristles

>> Spacing of bristles

Some have metal interiors or cores that retain heat to strengthen the curl pattern.

## COMBS

The main features of a comb are its size and the spacing between its teeth. Some combs have a pointed end, called the tail, which is used to part, lift or detail the hair. When a comb has widely spaced teeth, the resulting movement in the hair reflects the shape and interval of the teeth. Combs most often used in long hair design are:

### MASTER SKETCHER COMB

>> Large comb used to backcomb and smooth surface of hair

### MOLDING COMB

>> Used to distribute and mold hair

>> Used during finishing

### FINE-TOOTH TAIL COMB

>> Used for sectioning

>> Used during finishing and detailing

>> Also known as a drawing comb

### WIDE-TOOTH TAIL COMB

>> Used for backcombing and finishing techniques

## LONG HAIR TOOLS

| TOOLS | FUNCTION |
|---|---|
| Blow Dryer | Air forms wet hair while using brushes, combs and your fingers to create temporary direction and textural changes |
| Diffuser | Spreads gentle airflow to large area of hair; attachment for blow dryer |
| Concentrator | Focuses airflow to small area of hair; attachment for blow dryer |
| Curling Iron | Adds curled or waved texture to hair; utilizes a heated barrel powered by electric cord, base or stove |
| Flat Iron | Straightens and silks hair |
| Crimping Iron | Creates crimped or angular texture; sometimes used for base support |
| Air Forming Brush | Greater airflow; lengths can be dried quickly, into lines of design |
| Round Brush | Used to create volume and curved end texture |
| Cushion Brush | Relaxes sets, backbrushes, dry molds, defines the form |
| Fine-Tooth Tail Comb | Sections, parts and distributes the hair |
| Large-Tooth Tail Comb | Backcombs; used for finishing techniques |
| Master Sketcher Comb | Detangles and backcombs hair |

# LONG HAIR ESSENTIALS

To perform professional long hair services, you need a selection of products, supplies and equipment, in addition to tools. Long hair tools also include the tools that you'll use to properly prepare the hair prior to creating the long hair design, such as rollers and thermal irons. Properly preparing the hair sets the foundation to build upon. Once the hair is properly prepared, you will use a variety of combs, brushes, hairpins and finishing products, such as hairspray, to create your designs.

Corey Balazowich // CC BY-ND 2.0

## SUPPLIES

Elastic bands, bobby pins and hairpins support and secure long hair designs. Available in a wide variety of colors and sizes, they're often chosen to match the hair color to help conceal them. The design's ability to last through an event is essential. The design's strength, produced by bobby pins, hairpins and the base to which the lengths are secured, is usually hidden. It should appear weightless, as if defying gravity.

### Bobby Pins

>> Generally used to secure large or heavy sections to other areas

>> Pin usually opened slightly and then slid into hair to secure

>> Closed pin can also be used, depending on technique

*Locking*

>> Creates extra security

>> Bobby pins are crossed over one another

>> Especially useful to create lines of bobby pins

▪ E.g. vertical line of locked bobby pins used in vertical roll design

### Elastic Bands

>> Generally used to hold ponytails in position

>> Used to secure the ends of a braided or twisted strand

>> Covered hair bands can be gentler on hair

Designers usually prefer to use an elastic hair band with one or two bobby pins to secure a ponytail for a design.

### Hairpins

>> Used to secure smaller, more delicate areas

>> Easier to conceal

>> Often placed closer to surface of design

Longer hairpins are used to temporarily hold hair in place while working and are removed when the design is complete.

## Hairnets

>> Extra support and security in areas that are especially heavy or long

>> Also used to create fillers

---

## Fillers (Padding)

>> Provide shape and support in design

>> Often made from synthetic hair fibers; backcombed and placed into hairnet

>> Allow designer to customize shape and volume

>> Also called padding

Manufactured fillers come in a variety of different colors, shapes and materials.

## PRODUCTS

Long hair is exposed to more stress than shorter lengths, often resulting in dull, dry or unruly hair.

| **Natural Stress** | **Physical Stress** |
|---|---|
| >> Water | >> Thermal tools |
| >> Sunlight | >> Ponytails worn too often or too tight |

Using the right products at the right time can:

>> Tame unruly hair

>> Make hair look healthier

>> Add support and longevity to a design

Knowing which products to use when for the intended design will help you achieve beautiful results. Carefully choose which products to use:

>> Prior to air forming or setting

>> During air forming or setting

>> While designing or putting hair up

>> While finishing and detailing

PIVOT POINT FUNDAMENTALS: COSMETOLOGY | **108º.2 - 25**

The chart below gives general ideas about products to use with different natural hair textures and when to use them. In long hair design, tool and product selection is often based more on the desired texture than the natural texture of the hair.

| All Hair Types | >> Thermal Protective Spray – Before and during hair preparation<br>>> Working Hairspray – Before and during hair preparation and design<br>>> Finishing Hairspray – After design is complete<br>>> Shine Spray – During and after design |
|---|---|
| Fine-Medium Hair | >> Detangler – Before hair preparation<br>>> Mousse – Before hair preparation<br>>> Volumizing Spray – Before and during hair preparation<br>>> Pomade – During and after design |
| Medium-Coarse Hair | >> Leave-In Conditioner – Before hair preparation<br>>> Gel – Before hair preparation<br>>> Silicone Serum – Before and after hair preparation; during design<br>>> Wax – During and after design |

## LONG HAIR SUPPLIES

| SUPPLIES | FUNCTION |
|---|---|
| Bobby Pin | Secures hair in place for finished design, especially in long hair designs |
| Hairpin | Secures hair in place for finished design, especially in long hair designs |
| Long Hairpin | Defines textural detail and movement; controls formation of shapes while creating design; holds lengths in place temporarily; u-shaped hairpins with or without ridges |
| Elastic Band | Holds ponytails in position |
| Hairnet | Controls and secures hair design or portion of design; delicate, open-meshed fabric, usually knotted or woven and attached to fine elastic band |
| Filler | Expands design or creates specific forms using loose hair fiber |
| Hairpiece | Covers specific areas of head for definite purposes; used to add length, color or shape to design; made of human or artificial hair |
| Hair Form | Expands design by using fiber-filled shape |
| Hair Accessory | Provides ornamentation and/or method to secure hair; ranges from plastic combs to jewel-encrusted clips |

# LONG HAIR PRODUCTS

| PRODUCTS | FUNCTION |
| --- | --- |
| Detangler | Helps detangle wet hair |
| Mousse | Supports volume and movement; used to define texture and directional patterns; foam consistency; may contain conditioners |
| Volumizing Spray | Supports volume and movement; available in various consistencies |
| Styling Lotion | Supports volume and movement; liquid consistency |
| Spray Gel | Supports volume and movement; used for wet-look finishes; firmer hold than lotion; liquid consistency |
| Non-Aerosol Hairspray | Holds finished design in place; liquid dispensed through pump |
| Aerosol Hairspray | Holds finished design in place; available in a variety of strengths; liquid dispensed through compressed gas and spray |
| Pomade/Polisher | Adds high-intensity gloss and sheen; adds texture separation and definition; adds weight to hair |
| Shine Spray | Adds shine and provides hair control |
| Oil Sheen | Adds shine and provides hair control |
| Silicone Serum | Adds shine and provides hair control |
| Wax | Provides hair control; generally matte finish |

## DISCOVER**MORE**

Build your future by looking into the past! Research combs, accessories, tools and techniques from the past or from cultures other than your own. Discover how stunning long hair designs have been created without some of the things we take for granted and with materials that you might not think to use.

## LONG HAIR EQUIPMENT

| EQUIPMENT | FUNCTION |
|---|---|
| Hair Design Station | Provides a place for tools to be displayed and organized |
| Hydraulic Chair | Provides proper back support for client during service; adjustable |
| Wet Disinfectant Container | Holds solution for disinfecting tools |
| Shampoo Bowl | Supports client's neck and holds water and shampoo products during a shampoo service |
| Mirror | Displays hair design to client and hair designer for communication and balancing design |

### ALERT!

**Always follow manufacturer's directions for the proper use, disinfection and maintenance of long hair essentials.**

## SALON**CONNECTION**

### Expand Your Tool Kit

Salon stylists who excel in long hair design know that they need to have a wide range of specialized tools, products and supplies at their disposal.
You may have a "go-to" kit already, but be open to experiment with new tools and techniques for new effects—have fun while you're at it!

A working knowledge of the tools, supplies and products used in long hair design will help you create beautiful designs that fulfill your long hair clients' needs.

## LESSONS LEARNED

>> The main tools used in long hair design include:

**Thermal Tools**

- Blow Dryers – Used to air form wet hair

- Curling Irons, Flat Irons and Thermal Rollers – Used to create temporary hair texture changes

**Brushes**

- Air Forming Brushes – Allow greatest airflow to dry hair quickly

- Round Brushes – Create volume and curved end texture

- Cushion Brushes – Smooth hair and increase shine

**Combs**

- Master Sketcher Comb – Backcomb and smooth surface

- Molding Comb – Distribute, mold, finish

- Fine-Tooth Tail Comb – Section, finish, detail

- Wide-Tooth Tail Comb – Backcomb, finish

>> Supplies include bobby pins, hairpins, elastic bands, hairnets and fillers. These are used to secure elements of the design.

>> Products used for long hair design include gels, mousses, hairsprays and a variety of shine products.

>> Equipment includes permanent fixtures, such as the hair dressing station, hydraulic chair and shampoo bowl.

108ᶜ.3 //
# LONG HAIR SKILLS

## INSPIRE //

Following specific procedures will ensure your success with the long hair techniques you choose to perform for your clients.

## ACHIEVE //

Following this lesson on *Long Hair Skills*, you'll be able to:

>> State the importance of preparing the hair before creating a long hair design

>> Provide examples of the five long hair procedures used to ensure predictable results

>> Provide examples of the six common long hair techniques

## EXPLORE //

**How important do you think your technical skills are in gaining long hair referrals?**

## FOCUS //

**LONG HAIR SKILLS**
Long Hair Preparation
Long Hair Procedures
Long Hair Techniques

# 108<sup>c</sup>.3 |
# LONG HAIR SKILLS

Mastering long hair techniques and using organized,
efficient procedures will ensure that your results
match your clients' expectations every time.
While every design may not require every one
of the standard procedures, working in logical
sequence is just as critical to your success.

To create the design you have envisioned, you'll need to choose and
follow the proper steps to prepare the hair to move, bend or drape.
These preparation steps are followed by long hair procedures and
techniques, resulting in predictable long hair results.

# LONG HAIR PREPARATION

Experienced designers find that preparation saves time when putting the hair up, producing cleaner and more professional results.

Depending on the long hair design, the hair may be set to achieve smooth and straight, tightly curled, wavy or combinations of different textures. The pattern of the set should reflect the overall direction of the finished long hair design and direction within specific areas.

Tools, products and techniques used in wet and thermal hair designing may be applied when preparing long hair for an updo or a long hair style. This means that having solid skills in the wet and thermal hair designing will give you the best foundation for your long hair designs.

Below are just some of the common wet and thermal design techniques and tools used to prepare lengths for a long hair design.

## THERMAL ROLLERS

Large-diameter thermal rollers add body and curved texture to support this vertical roll design.

Setting the hair with thermal rollers, after it has been gathered into a ponytail, positions support and texture only where needed.

## THERMAL IRONS

A large-barrel curling iron used to curl from the midstrand to ends makes it easier to manipulate lengths and conceal flyaways.

For more defined texture, small sections are twisted and wrapped around the barrel of the curling iron.

## BLOW DRYER WITH ATTACHMENTS

Blow drying with a diffusor attachment enhances natural curls for a more casual feeling in this roll design.

A large diameter round brush along with a blow dryer and concentrator, smooths the cuticle for sleeker finishes with fewer flyaways.

# LONG HAIR PROCEDURES

Following a step-by-step procedure will ensure control of the form as you create a long hair design. Some or all of the long hair procedures can be used to organize your work and ensure the desired result. Several of these procedures are similar to the setting and finishing procedures used in hair design.

Once the desired shape, direction and position of volume are identified and the hair is properly prepared, you will put the hair up using the long hair design procedures:

| 1. Distribute | 2. Section | 3. Part | 4. Apply | 5. Detail |

 ## DISTRIBUTE

Distribution is used throughout the long hair design service and:

>> Defines the overall direction of the design

>> Determines the directions in which the eye travels throughout the design

>> Can lead the eye to a focal point

Overall, distribution is usually performed to prepare the hair for the position of ponytail(s) or volume. Options include distributing the hair:

>> Away from the face

>> Toward the crown

>> Toward the nape

>> Downward from a part

>> Upward from the nape

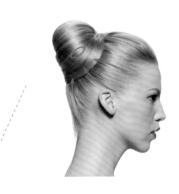

Distribution of individual strands or partings creates detail and movement that lead the eye through the design and create interest.

In the absence of a ponytail, distribution is generally performed in the direction the hair will be worn, including upward toward the crown, away from the face, or from a part.

## SECTION

In long hair designing, **sectioning** is used for control, separating areas of the design that will be treated with different techniques. Therefore, sectioning also influences the proportions within the design. The number of sections within a design depends on the intricacy desired in the results.

The initial sectioning often creates a base, such as a ponytail, or a seam with interlocking bobby pins. Proper sectioning will ensure that:

>> The base is positioned in the most favorable spot to continue building the design

>> The overall direction and placement of the focal point are accurate before proceeding

Sectioning options for long hair design include:

>> Front        >> Occipital        >> Fringe        >> Crown

>> Back         >> Hairline         >> Nape

The hair is often distributed within established sections to position ponytails. This results in a concentration of volume in those areas. In many instances, ponytails are then sectioned further before the long hair technique is applied.

Hair is distributed to nape to position one ponytail.

The ponytail is further sectioned to apply the twist technique.

A concentration of volume and mass is achieved in the nape.

Increase the number of ponytails or sections within a design to vary the position of volume and influence the shape.

Two sections each have a ponytail positioned within them.

The two ponytails are intertwined and secured around the bases of the ponytails.

An elongated diagonal concentration of volume is achieved in the back and nape.

If no ponytails are used, you may need to section as the design is being created to control the hair and the position of volume.

Sectioning helps the designer stay organized and follow the plan.

## PART

Partings are used to subdivide larger sections of hair for control. Specific long hair techniques are usually applied to individual partings, which, when combined, create the surface texture of the design.

In most cases, partings are chosen to work with the direction in which the hair will be distributed before securing.

Depending on the design, partings may be:

>> Straight          >> Curved

>> Zigzagged        >> Irregular

Distributing the hair neatly from partings is important for smooth, clean lines in the final look. Distribution from individual partings or shapes is performed in preparation for the chosen technique.

More partings will usually result in more:

>> Detail

>> Textural interest

>> Smaller individual shapes

### Examples:

A single ponytail divided into five partings creates fewer, larger shapes with moderate detail.

Many individual partings used to form loops throughout the interior create many smaller shapes and intricacy.

Partings that are exposed in the finished design can be an intentional visual aspect of a design.

## APPLY

Long hair techniques are applied after hair has been distributed, sectioned and parted as necessary. Foundational long hair techniques include:

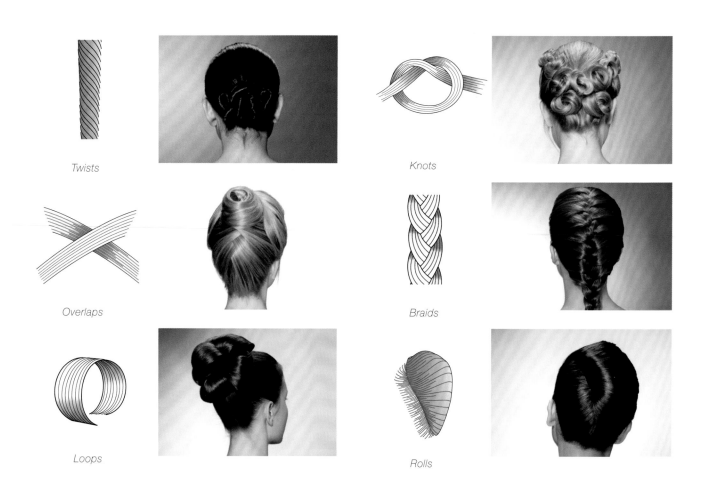

*Twists*

*Knots*

*Overlaps*

*Braids*

*Loops*

*Rolls*

The techniques chosen will determine whether the finished texture will be more smooth (unactivated) or patterned (activated).

## Backcombing/Backbrushing

Backcombing or backbrushing is an optional step to control the overall shape and individual shapes within a design, which gives them the ability to last. In most instances, backcombing and backbrushing are performed with loop and roll techniques to increase the amount of volume and strength of the shape(s). The surface of the hair is smoothed in the direction the hair will be worn without removing the support.

## Securing

Generally, hairpins and bobby pins are used to secure long hair. Usually they are intended to be concealed or hidden. To do this, position hairpins or bobby pins underneath the surface or within the shape.

Be aware of trends or specific fashion statements that may intentionally expose hairpins or bobby pins.

When a long hair design requires a ponytail, designers often prefer to secure with an elastic hair band and one or two bobby pins. This securing method:

>> Allows the hand controlling hair to stay in one position and tight against the head while securing

>> Avoids moving hair while securing

>> Keeps hair and ponytail smooth, tight and positioned correctly

**1-BOBBY-PIN TECHNIQUE**

Prepare elastic band by sliding one bobby pin through it. Gather hair with thumb up and hand close to head.

Hook elastic band around your thumb.

Hold bobby pin while wrapping band around hair.

Continue to wrap the band around hair. Then insert end of band that is wrapped around thumb into bobby pin.

Pull bobby pin up slightly, then turn it downward so that open end faces gathered hair and push under base of ponytail.

**2-BOBBY-PIN TECHNIQUE**

Prepare elastic hair band by sliding two bobby pins onto it. Gather hair into position holding hand close to head.

Insert one bobby pin at base of intended ponytail.

Push hand firmly against head to hold bobby pin in place while wrapping band around hair.

Push second pin into hair close to head interlocking first bobby pin in an "X" formation.

Hairpins are often used to secure smaller more delicate areas within a design.

Hairnets can also help secure areas that are especially heavy or long.

# DETAIL

Detailing refers to the finishing touches performed along the way, or during a final phase to personalize. Detailing in long hair design includes:

>> Refining

>> Smoothing stray hairs into place

>> Using finishing and shine sprays

>> Double-checking pins

Long hairpins are used to temporarily control shapes, textural detail and movements within a design. Once the hair is properly secured underneath the surface, the long hairpins are removed.

Detailing designs for special occasions may also include adding decorative pieces or accessories. These can be used both aesthetically and functionally to conceal hairpins and bobby pins, or in place of them.

When detailing:

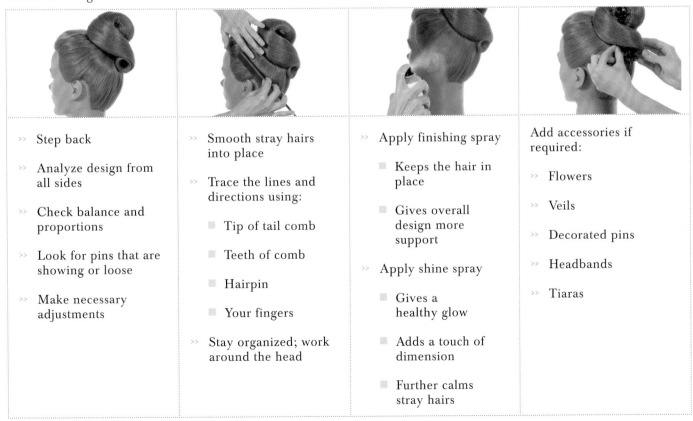

| | | | |
|---|---|---|---|
| >> Step back | >> Smooth stray hairs into place | >> Apply finishing spray | Add accessories if required: |
| >> Analyze design from all sides | >> Trace the lines and directions using: | ▪ Keeps the hair in place | >> Flowers |
| >> Check balance and proportions | ▪ Tip of tail comb | ▪ Gives overall design more support | >> Veils |
| >> Look for pins that are showing or loose | ▪ Teeth of comb | >> Apply shine spray | >> Decorated pins |
| >> Make necessary adjustments | ▪ Hairpin | ▪ Gives a healthy glow | >> Headbands |
| | ▪ Your fingers | ▪ Adds a touch of dimension | >> Tiaras |
| | >> Stay organized; work around the head | ▪ Further calms stray hairs | |

# SALON**CONNECTION**

### Design Decisions for Special Occasions

Many of your long hair clients will be headed for special occasions—possibly even their own weddings—and you may be asked to incorporate a hair accessory into your design. Keep an eye out for the latest trends in hair accessories and how they are being worn so you can make relevant, on-trend suggestions and recommendations for your clients.

## >> LONG HAIR TECHNIQUES

Your hands will be your primary tools to move, bend and weave hair to create long hair designs. Six basic long hair techniques are featured in this lesson: twists, knots, overlaps, braids, loops and rolls. These techniques can be performed off-the-scalp or directly on-the-scalp, creating unlimited design options.

Off-the-Scalp Designs – Created from ponytails

On-the-Scalp Designs – Created directly from the scalp

## TWISTS

The **twist** technique consists of strands of hair intertwined and/or rotated in clockwise or counterclockwise direction.

》 Create a rope-like appearance

》 May be applied on- or off-the-scalp with one, two, even three strands

》 Vary based on:

■ Tension

■ Size of strand(s)

■ Direction (clockwise, counterclockwise)

After twisting, the strand is usually arranged and placed to build a textured shape within the long hair design.

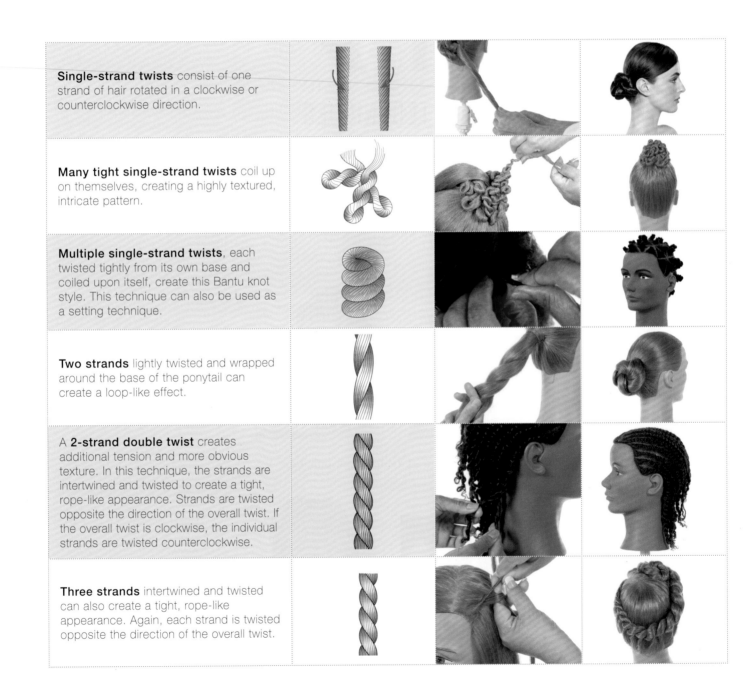

**Single-strand twists** consist of one strand of hair rotated in a clockwise or counterclockwise direction.

**Many tight single-strand twists** coil up on themselves, creating a highly textured, intricate pattern.

**Multiple single-strand twists**, each twisted tightly from its own base and coiled upon itself, create this Bantu knot style. This technique can also be used as a setting technique.

**Two strands** lightly twisted and wrapped around the base of the ponytail can create a loop-like effect.

A **2-strand double twist** creates additional tension and more obvious texture. In this technique, the strands are intertwined and twisted to create a tight, rope-like appearance. Strands are twisted opposite the direction of the overall twist. If the overall twist is clockwise, the individual strands are twisted counterclockwise.

**Three strands** intertwined and twisted can also create a tight, rope-like appearance. Again, each strand is twisted opposite the direction of the overall twist.

## KNOTS

The **knot** technique consists of the interlacing or tying together of one or two strands or partings to create a knot.

Knots can be:

>> Applied on or off the scalp

>> Tied in clockwise or counterclockwise directions

>> Applied to small individual partings for textural detail

>> Applied to larger sections to encompass larger areas of the head

>> Positioned along the base, midstrand, ends or any combination

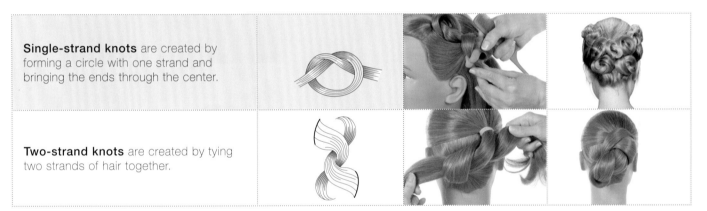

**Single-strand knots** are created by forming a circle with one strand and bringing the ends through the center.

**Two-strand knots** are created by tying two strands of hair together.

## OVERLAPS

The **overlap** technique is the crossing of two strands of hair in opposite directions, creating a crisscross effect. Clients will often refer to this technique as a fishtail braid, particularly when it is performed off-the-scalp.

» May be applied on- or off-the-scalp

» Commonly combined with other techniques to add interest

» Parting size will change the result of the design significantly

| | | | |
|---|---|---|---|
| Two strands alternately crossed over one another in a downward direction while projected away from the head can create a draped effect. | | | |
| The same technique worked close to the head creates a tighter silhouette. | | | |

## DISCOVER**MORE**

### Technique Connections
Do some research to find additional or variations of long hair techniques that are currently in high demand. See how they relate to the six core techniques in this lesson. Always look for techniques and ideas that will allow you to expand your offerings to your clients.

## BRAIDS

A **braid** consists of the crossing or weaving of three or more strands of hair. Twine, plait, pleat, weave, intertwine and interlock are just some of the terms used to describe the art of braiding throughout time.

**The two most common braiding methods are 3-strand overbraid, also known as the French or invisible braid, and the 3-strand underbraid, also known as the visible braid. The difference between the two techniques is whether a strand of hair is crossed over or under a center strand.**

Braids are classified according to the number of strands used, ranging from 3 to 5, 7, 9 or more. The 3-strand braid is the foundation of all braids. Once the 3-strand braid has been established, adjacent strands are woven toward the center. Any of these braids can be performed off-the-scalp in a ponytail or on-the-scalp. When creating a 5-strand braid, once the 3-strand braid is established, strands 4 and 5 are woven under the adjacent strand and over the center. When creating a 9-strand, "under, over, under, over" describes how strands 8 and 9 are woven toward the center strand.

### 3-Strand Overbraid

>> Outside strands are crossed *over* the center strand

>> Creates inverted appearance when performed on-the-scalp

>> Referred to as an invisible braid or French braid

>> Used to create one 3-strand braid that conforms to curve of head

>> Used for one or multiple braids

### 3-Strand Underbraid

>> Outside strands are crossed *under* the center strand

>> Referred to as a visible braid or Dutch braid

>> Creates a projected braid pattern when performed on-the-scalp

>> Used for one or multiple braids

Three-strand underbraids performed in small, often parallel sections, are also known as **cornrows**. Cornrowing can be a combination of on-the-scalp braiding that then extends off-the-scalp.

**Multiple-strand braids** create a wider pattern of intricate woven texture.

## LOOPS

The **loop technique** consists of folding, bending or encircling hairstrands, which are then secured in a curvature shape. Loops can be open or closed on one end or both. As the number of loops in the design increases, the pattern becomes more intricate. One large loop may also need a filler to support the shape.

To achieve a multitude of loop design possibilities, vary the:

>> Size
>> Dimension
>> Position
>> Shape

- Circular Loops – Rounded appearance
- Elongated Loops – Look cylindrical or triangular

### Single-Loop Technique

One strand of hair is used to form one loop.

### Double-Loop Technique

One strand of hair is used to form two loops.

## ROLLS

Rolls consist of hair that is wrapped or wound within itself. Rolls can be cylindrical or conical in shape and positioned along any line of the celestial axis. Rolls are typically the main feature in a design and sometimes incorporate all of the lengths. They also may be combined with other techniques.

The size and shape of the roll is determined by:

>> Fashion trends

>> Personal preference

>> The length of the client's hair

Being familiar with the specific options and procedures for long hair techniques will ensure predictable results and help you consistently satisfy your clients.

## LESSONS LEARNED

Preparing hair prior to performing a long hair design saves time and produces cleaner, more professional results. You should be purposeful in choosing and applying:

>> Products

>> Tools

>> Setting techniques

>> Patterns

The five long hair procedures are:

>> Distribute

>> Section

>> Part

>> Apply

>> Detail

The six long hair techniques are:

>> Twists

>> Knots

>> Overlaps

>> Braids

>> Loops

>> Rolls

# 108ᶜ.4 //
# LONG HAIR
## GUEST EXPERIENCE

What do you think would make a long hair client return to the same salon or stylist? What might make a client try a different salon or stylist?

## INSPIRE //

Offering exceptional guest experiences during long hair services will result in clients who return and refer new clients to you.

## ACHIEVE //

Following this lesson on *Long Hair Guest Experience*, you'll be able to:

>> Summarize the service essentials related to long hair designing

>> Restate in your own words the client considerations and communication guidelines used to ensure a successful long hair design

>> Provide examples of infection control and safety guidelines for long hair design services

## FOCUS //

**LONG HAIR GUEST EXPERIENCE**

Long Hair Service Essentials

Long Hair Client Considerations

Long Hair Infection Control and Safety

# 108ᶜ.4 | LONG HAIR GUEST EXPERIENCE

You want every service to be an outstanding experience for your long hair clients. Since many book their appointments for special occasions, you have the opportunity to contribute to memorable moments of their lives in profound ways.

## »» LONG HAIR SERVICE ESSENTIALS

All hair services require that you communicate with your client prior to the service to avoid misunderstandings and ensure predictable results. When discussing a long hair service with a client, use photos, magazines and idea boards to clarify their desires and your design intentions. When you reach a clear agreement on the service to be performed, you help manage expectations so they are more realistic and more likely to be met.

Refer to lessons on each of the four Service Essentials, *Design Connection* and *Client Considerations* for further guidelines.

## CONNECT

>> Meet and greet the client with a firm handshake and a pleasant tone of voice.

>> Communicate to build rapport and develop a relationship with the client.

## CONSULT

>> Ask questions to discover client needs, such as: "What is the event or special occasion you are attending?" "What role will you have in the event?" The answers to these questions will help you make the most appropriate design choices for your client.

>> Ask your client to describe what she will be wearing. Listen for details relating to lines, shapes patterns and textures.

>> Ask your client if she has any accessories that she would like to include in her long hair design, such as a veil or ornate hair clips.

>> Ask questions to determine the type of impression your client would like to convey for the occasion, which may have little to do with how she presents herself with her everyday look.

>> Ask questions to better understand your client's personality. This helps you create a design that the client will be comfortable wearing.

>> Analyze your client's face and body shape, physical features, hair and scalp. Consider volume placement from all angles, including the profile view. Refer to the *Client Considerations* lesson for further guidelines.

>> Assess the facts, visualize the end result and thoroughly think through your recommendations.

>> Explain your recommended services, solutions and their prices. You may also want to discuss the cost of any trial or practice sessions recommended.

>> Get feedback from your client and obtain consent before proceeding with the service.

## CREATE

>> Drape your client with a towel and plastic cape during the shampoo process for protection. Once the hair is properly dried, replace the plastic cape with a cloth cape for the actual long hair service. If the client has already shampooed in preparation for the appointment, begin with a cloth cape.

>> Ensure client comfort during the service.

>> Stay focused on delivering the long hair service to the best of your ability.

>> Teach the client how to use a light holding spray, if necessary, as the day and the event progress.

>> Teach the client how to take down the style after the event.

## COMPLETE

>> Request specific feedback from your client. Ask questions and look for verbal and nonverbal cues to determine your client's level of satisfaction.

>> Escort client to the retail area and show at least two products you used.

>> Invite your client to make a purchase.

>> Suggest a future appointment for your client's next special occasion.

>> Offer sincere appreciation to your client for visiting the school or salon.

>> Complete client record for future visits; include recommended products.

## » LONG HAIR CLIENT CONSIDERATIONS

Because long hair services are usually performed for special occasions, try to put extra focus and attention on exceeding client expectations by creating a beautiful, flattering and effective design. Communicate the relationship between the considerations discussed in this section and the completed long hair design to:

>> Help your client understand and accept your design recommendations

>> Build your professional reputation

>> Gain client trust and loyalty

>> Gain referrals that build your clientele

Here are some specific considerations to keep in mind as you communicate and work with your client to ensure that successful design decisions are made.

| | |
|---|---|
| FACIAL FEATURES | Based on your client's facial shape and her features, determine volume placement and whether detailing around the face is desirable. |
| | Soft or delicate features: |
| | >> Can be overpowered by too much detailing or hair around face |
| | >> Are often flattered by hair pulled off the face |
| | Bolder features: |
| | >> Can often carry off more detail around the face |
| | >> Hair can be used to balance or detract from features, such as a large nose or strong chin |
| BODY STRUCTURE | Identify your client's particular body shape and factor it into your design approach. Clients who are short and sturdy often benefit from a design with more height and volume, while the opposite is often true for tall and lanky clients. Refer to the *Client Considerations* lesson for additional information. |

| | |
|---|---|
| **HAIR LENGTH, DENSITY AND TEXTURE** | Analyze the condition of the hair to determine any limitations for the design. Clients with short hair who want an upswept design will present more limitations than those with longer lengths. For shorter-haired clients, hairpieces may be an option. Determine if the density and texture are sufficient to support the desired style. Specific products can be used to build up the hair, and fillers or padding can be used to support shapes. Refer to the *Wig, Hairpiece and Hair Addition Essentials* lesson for additional information. |
| **OCCASION** | Consider the nature and formality of the occasion, as well as your client's role in the event. Is she attending a wedding, or is she the bride-to-be? Are they attending a black-tie affair or a prom? Make sure that you understand your client's perception of these terms as you consult. Answers to these questions will guide you in your decision-making process. |
| **WARDROBE** | Consider what the client will be wearing.<br><br>» Look at the lines the garments create on the body, especially at the neckline.<br><br>» Evaluate the amount of volume, such as full sleeves or a full skirt. A strapless gown will offer you different design options than one with a high or closed neckline.<br><br>» Smooth, sleek fabrics may be complemented with smooth, controlled hair designs.<br><br>» Intricate, beaded or highly textured fabrics may lend themselves to more intricate, yet simple, hair designs.<br><br>» Based on a variety of factors, including your client's preferences, you may choose to harmonize or contrast with fabric texture or detail. |
| **IMPRESSION** | Find out what kind of impression your client wants to make. How do they want to be perceived at this event? Options might include:<br><br>» Elegant and sophisticated<br><br>» Soft and romantic<br><br>» Cutting-edge and fashion-forward |

In long hair design, there's always more than just one choice—the options are endless. Listen to your client to gain insight into their personality, fashion sense and perceptions of the "perfect" long hair design. Then, use your professional knowledge and skills to meet, and even exceed, your client's expectations with a long hair design she'll be thrilled with.

## DISCOVER**MORE**

Research trends in garments usually worn for formal events, and observe the variety of shapes and textures that are available. Try to determine what types of long hair designs you think would complement some of the garments you find. Don't be surprised if some of the fashion images you find also include some creative long hair inspiration!

## COMMUNICATION GUIDELINES

The following chart will help you respond to some of the most common client cues in a way that encourages client trust and open communication.

| CLIENT CUE | DESIGNER RESPONSE |
|---|---|
| *"Updos always give me a headache."* | "We don't want you to have a headache during this important event. During our trial run, you can tell me if anything feels uncomfortable–like the tightness of the ponytail, bobby pins that hurt or the overall weight and balance of the design. Resolving these issues during our trial run, will ensure your comfort without any concerns." |
| *"What do I need to do to prepare for the big day?"* | "Gather everything in one place that you need to bring to the salon the day before. When you shampoo your hair the evening before the appointment, apply conditioner only from the midstrand to the ends. This will keep more volume and shine where it's needed the most. Wear a shirt that buttons up so you don't jeopardize the design when you change clothes." |
| *"I'd like my hair to be styled half-up."* | "Okay. Let's make sure we're in agreement about how much hair will be up or down. Let's look at some pictures of designs that are partially up and partially down so I can get a better idea of the proportions you have in mind." |
| *"I think my hair is much finer than the hair in this picture, but I really love this design."* | "You're right. Your hair is quite different from the hair in this picture. There are several options we could try to achieve similar results. Show me what you like best about the design. I can modify the techniques used on your hair to create a similar texture but with less volume. If the silhouette or volume of the design is more appealing to you, different techniques or padding can be used to create a similar look." |

# SALON**CONNECTION**

### Attractive Referrals

Many long hair clients will come to you based on referrals. Make sure that each client has the kind of enjoyable, comfortable salon experience that will make them eager to return and more than happy to recommend your services and your salon.

## ›› LONG HAIR INFECTION CONTROL AND SAFETY

It's your responsibility as a professional to protect your client by following infection control and safety practices with any and all services you provide.

Cleaning is a process of removing dirt, debris and potential pathogens to aid in slowing the growth of pathogens. Cleaning is performed prior to disinfection procedures.

Disinfection methods kill certain pathogens (bacteria, viruses and fungi) with the exception of spores. Disinfectants are available in varied forms, including concentrate, liquid, spray or wipes that are approved EPA-registered disinfectants available for use in the salon industry. Immersion and the use of disinfecting spray or wipes are common practices when it comes to disinfecting tools, multi-use supplies and equipment in the salon. Be sure to follow the manufacturer's directions for mixing disinfecting solutions and contact time if applicable.

### CLEANING AND DISINFECTION GUIDELINES

Keep in mind that only nonporous tools, supplies and equipment can be disinfected. All porous items must be discarded after each use. Always follow your area's regulatory guidelines.

| TOOLS, SUPPLIES AND EQUIPMENT | CLEANING GUIDELINES | DISINFECTION GUIDELINES |
|---|---|---|
| **Combs and Brushes** | ›› Remove hair and debris.<br><br>›› Preclean with soap and water. | Immerse in an approved EPA-registered disinfectant solution. |
| **Thermal Tools:**<br>**Blow Dryer/**<br>**Attachments**<br>**Thermal Irons**<br>**Flat Irons**<br>**Thermal Rollers** | ›› Remove hair and wipe with damp cloth.<br><br>›› Remove buildup as often as necessary. | Disinfect unplugged electrical appliances by spraying or wiping with an approved EPA-registered disinfectant. |
| **Bobby Pins, Hairpins*** | ›› Dispose after use. | N/A |
| **Elastic Bands*** | ›› Dispose after use. | N/A |
| **Hairnets*** | ›› Dispose after use. | N/A |
| **Filler/Padding*** | ›› Dispose after use, unless purchased by client. | Cannot be disinfected. |
| **Cape (plastic/cloth)** | ›› Remove hair from cape.<br><br>›› Wash in machine with soap after each use. | Some regulatory agencies may require use of an approved EPA-registered disinfectant. |
| **Neckstrip** | ›› Dispose after use. | Cannot be disinfected. |

*Client will usually take these supplies with them as part of the style.*

Store disinfected tools and multi-use supplies in a clean, dry, covered container or cabinet.

# Alert!

If tools, multi-use supplies or equipment have come in contact with blood or body fluids, the following disinfection procedures must take place:

**》 Use an approved EPA-registered hospital disinfectant according to manufacturer's directions and as required by your area's regulatory agency.**

## CARE AND SAFETY

Follow infection control procedures for personal care and client safety guidelines before and during the long hair design service to ensure your safety and the client's while also contributing to the salon's care.

| Personal Care | | Client Care Prior to the Service | |
|---|---|---|---|
| | » Wear single-use gloves as required. | | » Be sure the cape stays in place and the client's arms are underneath the cape. |
| » Check that your personal standards of health and hygiene minimize the spread of infection. | » Check the scalp for any diseases or disorders. If any are evident, refer the client to a physician and do not proceed with the service. | » Protect the client's skin and clothing from water with a freshly laundered towel and a freshly laundered plastic or waterproof cape. | » Handle tools with care to ensure your safety and that of your clients. |
| » Wash hands and dry thoroughly with a single-use towel. | » Refer to your area's regulatory agency for proper mixing/handling of disinfectant solutions. | » Protect the client's skin and clothing by replacing towel with a neck strip following the shampoo service, if performed. | » If any tools are dropped on the floor, be sure to pick them up, then clean and disinfect. |
| » Disinfect workstation.<br><br>» Clean and disinfect tools appropriately. | » Minimize fatigue by maintaining good posture during the service. | » Protect client's skin and clothing with neck strip and styling cape. | » Complete the client record, noting scalp/hair condition. |

## Client Care During the Service

- Be cautious and avoid scratching moles and skin tags.

- If you injure the client or yourself, immediately apply first-aid procedures.
  - If wound or burn is deep, stop service immediately, and seek emergency medical attention.

- Work carefully around nonremovable jewelry and piercings.

- Avoid discomfort of long hair falling into client's face or eyes.

- Be aware of nonverbal cues the client may be conveying.

- Be aware of scalp sensitivity while combing, crushing or styling client's hair.

- Store soiled towels in a dry, covered receptacle until laundered.

- Be aware of any sensitivity to tightness of ponytails or positioning of bobby pins or hairpins.

## Salon Care

- Ensure electrical cords are properly positioned to avoid accidental falls.

- Follow your area's health and safety guidelines, including cleaning and disinfecting procedures.

- Ensure electrical equipment, plugs and cables are in good condition, and remember to turn off after use.

- Ensure equipment, including the salon chair and shampoo chair, is clean and disinfected.

- Sweep or vacuum and dispose of hair clippings at the end of the service.

- Promote a professional image by ensuring your workstation is clean and tidy throughout the service.

- Report malfunctioning furniture/equipment to manager.

- Disinfect all tools after each use. Always use disinfected combs and brushes for each client.

- Clean/mop water spillage from floor to avoid accidental falls.

Communicating with your clients about their expectations and desires for their long hair design, then focusing on making the look suitable for the occasion will result in return clients and client referrals.

# LESSONS LEARNED

>> The service essentials related to long hair design can be summarized as follows:

- Connect – Meeting and greeting the client to build rapport

- Consult – Asking questions to discover client needs; analyzing client's face, body shape, physical features, hair and scalp; asking questions relating to occasion, wardrobe, accessories and desired impression; assessing the facts to make recommendations; explaining design options and gaining feedback and consent to move forward

- Create – Ensuring client safety and comfort; staying focused to deliver the best service; teaching and explaining products to your client; teaching client how to maintain the style during the event and how to take it down after the event

- Complete – Requesting specific feedback; showing at least three products; suggesting future appointment times; completing client records

>> Some of the client considerations and communication guidelines that help ensure successful long hair designs include:

| | |
|---|---|
| Facial features | Occasion |
| Body structure | Wardrobe |
| Hair length, texture and density | Impression |

>> Infection control and safety guidelines must be followed throughout a long hair service to ensure your safety and the safety of the clients and the salon. Disinfectants are available in varied forms, including concentrate, liquid, spray, wipes that have EPA approval for use in the salon industry. Be guided by your area's regulatory agency for proper cleaning and disinfection guidelines.

# 108<sup>c</sup>.5 //
# LONG HAIR SERVICE

## EXPLORE //

**Have you ever been to the salon and felt like your stylist took shortcuts or didn't put in their full effort?**

## INSPIRE //

Following long hair procedures throughout the service results in a smooth and organized client experience—ensuring success with each client and generating referrals.

## ACHIEVE //

Following this lesson on *Long Hair Service*, you'll be able to:

>> Provide examples of procedural guidelines to follow when performing a long hair service

>> Describe the three areas of a long hair service

## FOCUS //

**LONG HAIR SERVICE**

Long Hair Client Guidelines

Long Hair Service Overview

Long Hair Rubric

# 108ᶜ.5 | LONG HAIR SERVICE

Procedures may not seem exciting, but they give you a framework to apply your creativity and technical skills and achieve predictable results. You'll have the confidence to explore and build your long hair repertoire.

In this lesson, it all comes together— everything you have learned about long hair theory, tools, skills and the guest experience. The safety and satisfaction of your client is ensured when you apply this knowledge before, during and after each long hair service.

# LONG HAIR CLIENT GUIDELINES

Now that you have a thorough understanding of long hair theory, you're ready to begin applying your knowledge to the medium of hair. Combining techniques within a design will allow you to create an infinite variety of looks for your clients. However, the finished result is not the only thing your client will remember.

The following chart will help ensure your client's comfort and safety during the long hair service.

| | | |
|---|---|---|
| **DISTRIBUTE** | | » Turn client to side:<br>▪ Distribute hair to different areas of head<br>▪ Analyze profile in mirror<br>▪ Assess most flattering distribution and placement of volume<br>» If a ponytail is used to establish a base for the long hair design:<br>▪ Ask client if she feels pulling or discomfort<br>▪ Loosen ponytail slightly to relieve discomfort before proceeding |
| **SECTION** | | » Section and clip areas of hair, as necessary:<br>▪ To stay organized<br>▪ To keep design balanced<br>» Conceal sectioning lines as much as possible, unless visible sectioning lines are part of design. |
| **PART** | | » Determine number of partings:<br>▪ Based on how intricate or "busy" intended design is<br>▪ Balance with texture of wardrobe<br>» For looser, more lived-in designs, partings can be taken with your fingers rather than a tail comb. |
| **APPLY** | | » Use a "working" hairspray while applying long hair techniques to individual partings:<br>▪ Use sparingly, as needed<br>▪ Avoid spraying too close to hair<br>▪ Ensure styling product itself is not visible on hair<br>» Ask client to inform you if a bobby pin or hairpin causes discomfort:<br>▪ Make adjustments to relieve discomfort |
| **DETAIL** | | » Use long hairpins to position and hold hair in place while working:<br>▪ Remember overall feeling of look to avoid overworking and becoming too perfect or clean<br>▪ Make sure detailing is balanced throughout<br>» Use finishing and shine spray after application and detailing:<br>▪ To strengthen style's ability to last<br>▪ For a firm, polished finish<br>▪ Only if desired or needed |

# LONG HAIR SERVICE OVERVIEW

The long hair procedures include attention to the four Cs.

**CONNECT**
>> Greet the client and communicate.

>> Build rapport and develop a relationship.

**CONSULT**
>> Ask questions to discover client's wants and needs.

>> Analyze the hair and scalp and check for any contraindications.

>> Introduce products and teach their benefit.

>> Gain consent before proceeding with the service.

**CREATE**
>> Ensure client protection and comfort.

>> Create predictable long hair results.

**COMPLETE**
>> Share appropriate follow-up care.

The Long Hair Service Overview identifies the three areas of every long hair service:

>> The Long Hair Preparation provides a brief overview of the steps to follow *before* you actually begin the long hair design.

>> The Long Hair Procedure provides an overview of the five steps/techniques that you will use *during* the long hair design to ensure predictable results.

>> The Long Hair Completion provides an overview of the steps to follow *after* performing the long hair design to ensure guest satisfaction.

## DISCOVER**MORE**

### Stand Out!

Do some research online or by talking with salon stylists that you know to discover additional procedural steps that might be included during long hair appointments to make them outstanding and unique. You may find some ideas and tips that you'll want to incorporate into your own work.

## LONG HAIR SERVICE OVERVIEW

| LONG HAIR PREPARATION | |
|---|---|
| **LONG HAIR PREPARATION** | >> Clean and disinfect workstation. |
| | >> Arrange long hair essentials, including hairpins, bobby pins, elastic bands, combs, brushes, accessories, hairspray and shine spray. |
| | >> Wash your hands. |
| | >> Perform analysis of hair and scalp. |
| | >> Ask client to remove jewelry, and store it in a secure place. |
| | >> Drape client for a wet service, if hair is to be shampooed first; if not, drape for dry service. |

**LONG HAIR PROCEDURE**

>> Shampoo, condition and dry client's hair, unless client's hair is better to style when shampooed the day before.

>> Replace client's draping with cloth cape and neck strip once hair is dried, if applicable.

>> Perform long hair procedures to achieve desired results:

1. **Distribute** hair to reflect overall direction of design (away from face, toward crown, toward nape, downward from a part).
2. **Section** hair into workable areas for purpose of control (one or multiple ponytails, ponytail with perimeter lengths left free, individual partings with no ponytails).
3. **Part** hair in appropriate parting pattern (any straight or curved line from celestial axis).
4. **Apply** appropriate long hair techniques, and secure hair to achieve desired results (twists, knots, overlaps, braids, loops or rolls).
5. **Detail** hair (ensure hairpins and bobby pins are properly concealed; include ornamentation when applicable; control flyaways; use shine spray, hairspray).

>> Check form for balance (symmetrical or asymmetrical; flattering to client's head shape, face shape and profile).

**LONG HAIR COMPLETION**

>> Reinforce client's satisfaction with overall salon experience.

>> Make professional product recommendations.

>> Prebook client's next appointment.

>> End client's visit with warm and personal goodbye.

>> Discard single-use supplies, disinfect tools and multi-use supplies, disinfect workstation and arrange in proper order.

>> Complete client record.

# LONG HAIR RUBRIC

A performance rubric is a document that identifies defined criteria at which levels of performance can be measured objectively. The Long Hair Rubric is an example that your instructor might choose to use for scoring. The Long Hair Rubric is divided into three main areas—Preparation, Procedure, Completion. Each area is further divided into step-by-step procedures that will ensure client safety and satisfaction.

# LONG HAIR RUBRIC

Allotted Time: 1 Hour

Student Name:_____ ID Number: _____

Instructor: _____ Date: _____ Start Time: _____ End Time: _____

LONG HAIR SERVICE (Live Model) – *Each scoring item is marked with either a "Yes" or "No." Each "Yes" counts for one point. Total number of points attainable is 33 if shampoo and condition procedures are carried out. If not, total possible score is 31.*

| CRITERIA | YES | NO | INSTRUCTOR ASSESSMENT |
|---|:---:|:---:|---|
| **PREPARATION:** *Did student...* | | | |
| 1. Clean and set up workstation with properly labeled supplies? | ☐ | ☐ | |
| 2. Place disinfected tools and supplies at a visibly clean workstation? | ☐ | ☐ | |
| 3. Wash their hands? | ☐ | ☐ | |
| *Connect: Did student...* | | | |
| 4. Meet and greet client with a welcoming smile and pleasant tone of voice? | ☐ | ☐ | |
| 5. Properly drape client and prepare for service? | ☐ | ☐ | |
| 6. Communicate to build rapport and develop a relationship with client? | ☐ | ☐ | |
| 7. Refer to client by name throughout service? | ☐ | ☐ | |
| *Consult: Did student...* | | | |
| 8. Ask questions to discover client's wants and needs? | ☐ | ☐ | |
| 9. Analyze client's hair and scalp and check for any contraindications? | ☐ | ☐ | |
| 10. Gain feedback and consent from client before proceeding? | ☐ | ☐ | |
| **PROCEDURE:** *Did student...* | | | |
| 11. Ensure client protection and comfort by maintaining cape on outside of chair at all times? | ☐ | ☐ | |
| 12. If applicable, carry out appropriate shampoo and condition procedures? | ☐ | ☐ | |
| 13. Use products economically? | ☐ | ☐ | |
| 14. If applicable, replace client's draping with cloth cape and neck strip once hair was dried? | ☐ | ☐ | |
| *Create: Did student...* | | | |
| 15. Distribute hair to reflect overall direction of design? | ☐ | ☐ | |
| 16. Section hair into workable areas for control? | ☐ | ☐ | |
| 17. Part hair in appropriate parting pattern? | ☐ | ☐ | |
| 18. Apply appropriate long hair techniques and secure hair? | ☐ | ☐ | |
| 19. Detail hair? | ☐ | ☐ | |
| 20. Check form for balance? | ☐ | ☐ | |
| **COMPLETION (Complete):** *Did student...* | | | |
| 21. Maintain neck strip or towel and cape protection throughout service? | ☐ | ☐ | |
| 22. Practice infection control procedures safely throughout service? | ☐ | ☐ | |
| 23. Remove loose hairs from skin, cape and work area? | ☐ | ☐ | |
| 24. Sweep or vacuum hair from floor completely? | ☐ | ☐ | |
| 25. Discard nonreusable materials; disinfect tools and multi-use supplies; arrange workstation in proper order? | ☐ | ☐ | |
| 26. Maintain workspace that was safe, neat and clean throughout service? | ☐ | ☐ | |
| 27. Ask questions and look for verbal and nonverbal cues to determine client's level of satisfaction? | ☐ | ☐ | |
| 28. Make professional product recommendations? | ☐ | ☐ | |
| 29. Ask client to prebook a future appointment? | ☐ | ☐ | |
| 30. End guest's visit with a warm and personal goodbye? | ☐ | ☐ | |
| 31. Complete service within scheduled time? | ☐ | ☐ | |
| 32. Complete client record? | ☐ | ☐ | |
| 33. Wash their hands following the service? | ☐ | ☐ | |

COMMENTS: _____

_____

TOTAL POINTS = _____ ÷ 33 = _____ %

*\* If client's hair is not shampooed prior to the updo, the total possible score is 31.*

## LESSONS LEARNED

## SALON**CONNECTION**

### It's About Time...

Many of your long hair clients will be on a schedule for the day of a special event. Working efficiently and effectively by following procedures will help you stay within appointment times and keep your clients on schedule!

Procedural guidelines to follow when performing a long hair service to ensure client safety and satisfaction include:

» Distributing client's hair to different areas of the head to assess most flattering distribution and placement of volume

» Loosening a ponytail slightly to relieve discomfort if needed

» Sectioning and clipping hair to stay organized and keep design balanced

» Determining the appropriate number of partings for the intended design

» Determining whether a tail comb or fingers are used to part the hair

» Adjusting bobby pins or hairpins to relieve discomfort

» Detailing and finishing with appropriate products

» The three areas of a long hair service include Preparation, Procedure and Completion:

▪ Preparation – Includes setting up the workstation with disinfected tools and supplies; connecting with the client; properly draping the client

▪ Procedure – Includes ensuring client safety, shampooing/conditioning the client's hair, and creating the long hair design

▪ Completion – Includes infection control procedures, such as discarding single-use supplies and arranging/disinfecting workstation, determining client's level of satisfaction, recommending products, asking client to make a future appointment, ending guest's visit with a warm and personal goodbye and completing the client record

# SINGLE-STRAND TWISTS

### EXPLORE

**Do you think creating this design will be as intricate as it looks? Why?**

### INSPIRE

Intricate-looking designs are easily achieved with single-strand twists.

### ACHIEVE

Following this *Single-Strand Twists Workshop*, you'll be able to:

>> Identify the long hair procedures related to the single-strand twist design

>> Create a well-balanced design that incorporates single-strand twists from a ponytail

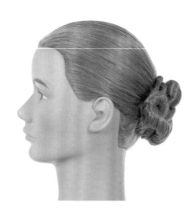

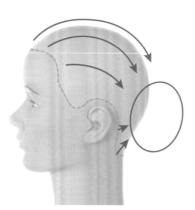

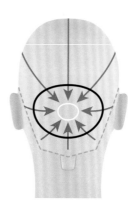

Twisted strands are positioned to create an interesting chignon.

Distribution is away from the face and volume is positioned in the nape.

The hair is distributed toward the nape to position the ponytail.

## LONG HAIR DESIGN PROCEDURES

1. DISTRIBUTE

2. SECTION

3. PART

4. APPLY

5. DETAIL

# SINGLE-STRAND TWISTS

Draw or fill in the boxes with the appropriate answers.

## DESIGN DECISIONS

### OVERALL SHAPE, POSITION OF VOLUME AND DIRECTION OF DESIGN

| FRONT | RIGHT | LEFT | BACK |
|-------|-------|------|------|

### PREPARE

☐ BLOW DRY STRAIGHT

☐ BLOW DRY ROUND BRUSH

☐ FLAT IRON

☐ CURLING IRON

☐ THERMAL ROLLERS

PRODUCTS/SUPPLIES

_____

_____

_____

### DISTRIBUTE

| TOP | RIGHT | LEFT | BACK |
|-----|-------|------|------|

### SECTION AND PART

| TOP | RIGHT | LEFT | BACK |
|-----|-------|------|------|

### APPLY

☐　　☐　　☐　　☐　　☐

**Instructor Signature** _____ **Date** _____

PERFORMANCE GUIDE

# SINGLE-STRAND TWISTS

View the video, complete the Design Decisions chart, then perform this workshop. Complete the self-check as you progress through the workshop.

**20 mins**
Suggested Salon Speed

| | | ✔ |
|---|---|---|
| **PREPARATION** | | |
| | » Assemble tools and products<br>» Set up workstation | ☐ |
| **HAIR PREPARATION – LONG SOLID LENGTHS** | | |
| | » Air form hair straight, away from face, toward position of ponytail | ☐ |
| **DISTRIBUTE** | | |
| | 1. **Distribute hair toward nape to prepare to position ponytail:**<br>» Distribute hair from front hairline, sides and perimeter toward nape | ☐ |
| | 2. **Secure ponytail using one-bobby-pin technique.** | ☐ |
| **SECTION/APPLY** | | |
| | 3. **Divide ponytail into three equal strands:**<br>» Clip two right strands | ☐ |
| | 4. **Twist left strand clockwise:**<br>» Twist from base to ends<br>» Apply medium tension | ☐ |

5. **Secure twisted left strand with bobby pins at base of ponytail:**

   » Wrap twisted strand upward and clockwise around base of ponytail

6. **Twist center strand counterclockwise.**

7. **Secure twisted center strand with bobby pins (in desired area):**

   » Direct center strand upward, then encourage coiled effect

8. **Form flat loop with ends; tuck and secure.**

9. **Twist third strand clockwise.**

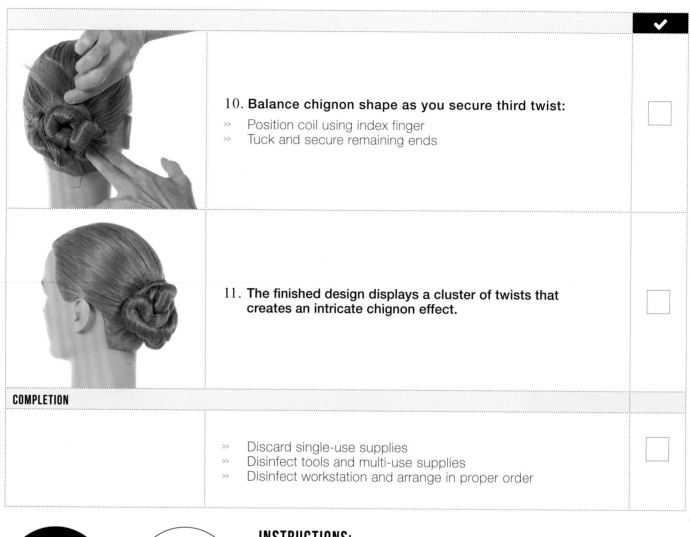

10. **Balance chignon shape as you secure third twist:**

  » Position coil using index finger
  » Tuck and secure remaining ends

11. **The finished design displays a cluster of twists that creates an intricate chignon effect.**

**COMPLETION**

  » Discard single-use supplies
  » Disinfect tools and multi-use supplies
  » Disinfect workstation and arrange in proper order

**20 mins**
Suggested Salon Speed

**My Speed**
———
———
———

**INSTRUCTIONS:**

Record your time in comparison with the suggested salon speed. Then, list here how you could improve your performance.

_____
_____
_____
_____
_____

**VARIATION – 2-STRAND TWISTS**

A variation of the single-strand twists design is available online. In this variation, the 2-strand twist technique is performed with light tension to create the illusion of loops.

## 2-STRAND OVERLAP

### EXPLORE

**Why do you think the 2-strand overlap, or "fishtail braid" is popular with celebrities and clients?**

### INSPIRE

The 2-strand overlap technique allows you to create a variety of designs that feature the "fishtail" look that is popular with clients.

### ACHIEVE

Following this *2-Strand Overlap Workshop*, you'll be able to:

>> Identify the long hair procedures related to the 2-strand overlap design

>> Create a well-balanced design using the 2-strand overlap technique through the center back

>> Maintain closeness to the head and use the correct finger positions while alternating hands as you work

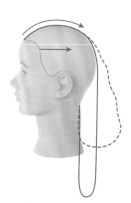

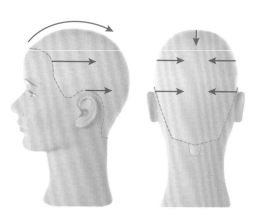

A 2-strand overlap is a great alternative to a traditional braid when a looser, more romantic finish is desired.

Distribution is back, off the face. Volume is at the nape when hanging lengths are tucked under. Minimal volume is achieved and the form is elongated when the overlapped lengths are worn down.

The hair is initially distributed to the crown, then toward the center back.

## LONG HAIR DESIGN PROCEDURES

1. DISTRIBUTE

2. SECTION

3. PART

4. APPLY

5. DETAIL

# 2-STRAND OVERLAP

Draw or fill in the boxes with the appropriate answers.

## DESIGN DECISIONS

### OVERALL SHAPE, POSITION OF VOLUME AND DIRECTION OF DESIGN

| FRONT | RIGHT | LEFT | BACK |

### PREPARE

PRODUCTS/SUPPLIES

☐ BLOW DRY STRAIGHT    ☐ FLAT IRON

☐ BLOW DRY ROUND BRUSH    ☐ CURLING IRON

☐ THERMAL ROLLERS

_____

_____

_____

### DISTRIBUTE

| TOP | RIGHT | LEFT | BACK |

### SECTION AND PART

| TOP | RIGHT | LEFT | BACK |

### APPLY

☐   ☐   ☐   ☐   ☐

---

**Instructor Signature** _____    **Date** _____

PERFORMANCE GUIDE

# 2-STRAND OVERLAP

View the video, complete the Design Decisions chart, then perform
this workshop. Complete the self-check as you progress through
the workshop.

**30
mins**
Suggested
Salon Speed

| PREPARATION | ✔ |
|---|---|
| >> Assemble tools and products<br>>> Set up workstation | ☐ |

### HAIR PREPARATION – LONG SOLID LENGTHS

| | |
|---|---|
| >> Air form hair back, away from face, toward center back<br>>> Curl ends with curling iron<br>>> Clip curls to cool completely<br>>> Relax set<br>>> Apply small amount of smoothing cream through the lengths | ☐ |

### DISTRIBUTE/SECTION

| | |
|---|---|
| 1. **Begin the 2-strand overlap with a horizontal horseshoe-shaped section:**<br>>> Distribute lengths back off face toward crown<br>>> Take horizontal horseshoe-shaped section at front hairline from center of each eyebrow to crown | ☐ |

### APPLY (TOP)

| | |
|---|---|
| 2. **Divide horseshoe-shaped section in half:**<br>>> Direct lengths straight back<br>>> Divide from front apex to crown<br>>> Cross left portion over to right | ☐ |
| 3. **Establish 2-strand overlap:**<br>>> Take small horizontal parting on right side<br>>> Cross this strand over and to inside of left section<br><br>>> Take a small horizontal parting on left side<br>>> Cross this strand to inside of right section<br>>> Use comb to distribute as needed | ☐ |

4. **Perform on-the-scalp 2-strand overlap:**
   - >> Horizontal partings will be used on either side

5. **Apply 2-strand overlap through crown:**
   - >> Take approximately ½" (1.25 cm) horizontal parting on left side; cross to inside of right strand
   - >> Switch hands and repeat on right side, crossing to inside of left strand
   - >> Hold hair with index finger between strands, middle finger against scalp, thumb for tension

## APPLY (SIDES)

6. **Work through sides:**
   - >> Alternate sides and hands
   - >> Take consistent ½" (1.25 cm) partings, working toward ear
   - >> Keep hands close to head for close shape
   - >> Control lengths being picked up with pinky finger before crossing over

## APPLY (NAPE)

7. **Continue overlap technique through nape:**
   - >> Horizontal partings

   **Note:** You may choose to work with your hands only as you work toward the nape area.

## APPLY (OFF-THE-SCALP)

8. **Apply off-the-scalp overlap technique:**
   - >> Small sections taken from outside, crossed to inside of opposite side
   - >> Smooth strands before crossing over
   - >> Keep strand size consistent; work toward ends

   **Note:** Sections should be no more than ¼ of the entire section.

**9. Work to ends using same technique:**
>> Secure with elastic band

**DETAIL**

**10. Loosen strands for contemporary finish:**
>> Work off-scalp from bottom of hanging lengths
   - Begin on one side; gently pull strands along outside
   - Check for balance; readjust as needed
>> Work on-scalp in similar fashion
   - From bottom to top

**11. Detail on-the-scalp lengths using hairpins.**

**12. The initial finish shows hair directed back, off the face with the overlap texture through the center back.**

**13. Further loosen strands for intentional, "undone" effect:**
>> Pull individual hair ends out gently
>> Work upward and check for balance
>> Work through on-the-scalp area in similar fashion

14. **Tuck and pin hanging lengths:**

>> Slightly backcomb ends below elastic band
>> Insert large bobby pin into elastic band
>> Turn ends up and under
>> Secure at nape
>> Apply second bobby pin from other side, crisscrossing first
>> Detail and expand further

15. **This finished design shows the characteristic crisscross effect of the 2-strand overlap technique softened by a looser surface texture, with the hanging lengths tucked at the nape to create more volume and less elongation.**

## COMPLETION

>> Discard single-use supplies
>> Disinfect tools and multi-use supplies
>> Disinfect workstation and arrange in proper order

**30 mins**
Suggested Salon Speed

**My Speed**

### INSTRUCTIONS:

Record your time in comparison with the suggested salon speed. Then, list here how you could improve your performance.

# 3-STRAND OVERBRAID

## EXPLORE

**How has the use of the classic French braid evolved in fashion over the years?**

## INSPIRE

You can create a wide range of looks—from classic to editorial—with the 3-strand overbraid technique.

## ACHIEVE

Following this *3-Strand Overbraid Workshop*, you'll be able to:

» Identify the long hair procedures related to the 3-strand overbraid

» Create a 3-strand on-the-scalp overbraid design with even tension and consistent partings throughout

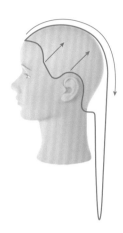

Although popular for younger clients, the 3-strand overbraid can be beautifully adapted to create fashionable adult looks.

The 3-strand overbraid begins at the front hairline and progresses to the nape. Lengths are distributed while partings are taken toward the center.

# LONG HAIR DESIGN PROCEDURES

1. DISTRIBUTE

2. SECTION

3. PART

4. APPLY

5. DETAIL

DESIGN DECISIONS CHART

# 3-STRAND OVERBRAID

Draw or fill in the boxes with the appropriate answers.

## DESIGN DECISIONS

### OVERALL SHAPE, POSITION OF VOLUME AND DIRECTION OF DESIGN

| FRONT | RIGHT | LEFT | BACK |
|-------|-------|------|------|

### PREPARE

☐ BLOW DRY STRAIGHT     ☐ FLAT IRON

☐ BLOW DRY ROUND BRUSH     ☐ CURLING IRON

☐ THERMAL ROLLERS

PRODUCTS/SUPPLIES

_____

_____

_____

### DISTRIBUTE

| TOP | RIGHT | LEFT | BACK |
|-----|-------|------|------|

### SECTION AND PART

| TOP | RIGHT | LEFT | BACK |
|-----|-------|------|------|

### APPLY

☐     ☐     ☐     ☐     ☐

**Instructor Signature** _____ **Date** _____

# 3-STRAND OVERBRAID

View the video, complete the Design Decisions chart, then perform this workshop. Complete the self-check as you progress through the workshop.

**20 mins**
Suggested Salon Speed

| **PREPARATION** | | ✔ |
|---|---|---|
| | >> Assemble tools and products<br>>> Set up workstation | ☐ |

| **HAIR PREPARATION – LONG SOLID LENGTHS** | | |
|---|---|---|
| | >> Blow dry hair straight, away from face<br>>> Apply appropriate products<br>>> Use paddle brush or large round brush | ☐ |

| **DISTRIBUTE/SECTION** | | |
|---|---|---|
| | 1. **Begin 3-strand overbraid with crescent-shaped section:**<br>>> Distribute lengths straight back<br>>> Take crescent-shaped section at front hairline<br>>> Divide crescent-shaped section into 3 equal strands | ☐ |

| **PART/APPLY** | | |
|---|---|---|
| | 2. **Cross left strand over center:**<br>>> Palm-up position | ☐ |
| | 3. **Cross right strand over center:**<br>>> Complete 3-strand sequence<br><br>**Note:** It is acceptable to cross the right or left strand over the center first, as long as you are consistent throughout. | ☐ |

4. Repeat, crossing left strand over center.

5. Take diagonal parting on left side and join section to center strand.

6. **Repeat same procedure on right side:**
>> Switch hands
>> Always hold strands you last crossed in one hand

7. **Work from side to side using same technique:**
>> Pick up consistent partings
>> Conform partings to curve of head

8. **Maintain tension working along curve of head:**
>> Tilt head forward slightly
>> Conform your hands to curve of head

9. **Work off-scalp:**
   >> Continue crossing left over center and right over center
   >> Work toward ends
   >> Secure with elastic band

10. **The finish shows a contoured overbraid with an elongated form.**

**COMPLETION**

>> Discard single-use supplies
>> Disinfect tools and multi-use supplies
>> Disinfect workstation and arrange in proper order

**20 mins**
Suggested Salon Speed

My Speed

**INSTRUCTIONS:**
Record your time in comparison with the suggested salon speed. Then, list here how you could improve your performance.

# 3-STRAND UNDERBRAID

### EXPLORE

**How would you describe the difference between an underbraid and an overbraid to a client?**

### INSPIRE

Being skilled in creating underbraid designs allows you to offer a whole new range of braiding styles to your clients.

### ACHIEVE

Following this *3-Strand Underbraid Workshop*, you'll be able to:

» Identify the long hair procedures related to the 3-strand underbraid

» Create a 3-strand on-the-scalp underbraid design with even tension and consistent partings throughout

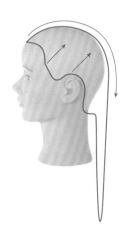

The underbraiding technique creates a braid that is visible or projected in appearance. This braid is sometimes referred to as a Dutch braid.

The 3-strand underbraid begins at the front hairline and progresses to the nape, creating an elongated shape. Lengths are distributed toward the center. Diagonal partings are taken at the sides.

# LONG HAIR DESIGN PROCEDURES

1. DISTRIBUTE

2. SECTION

3. PART

4. APPLY

5. DETAIL

DESIGN DECISIONS CHART

# 3-STRAND UNDERBRAID

Draw or fill in the boxes with the appropriate answers.

## DESIGN DECISIONS

### OVERALL SHAPE, POSITION OF VOLUME AND DIRECTION OF DESIGN

| FRONT | RIGHT | LEFT | BACK |
|-------|-------|------|------|

### PREPARE

☐ BLOW DRY STRAIGHT          ☐ FLAT IRON

☐ BLOW DRY ROUND BRUSH          ☐ CURLING IRON

☐ THERMAL ROLLERS

PRODUCTS/SUPPLIES

_____

_____

_____

### DISTRIBUTE

| TOP | RIGHT | LEFT | BACK |
|-----|-------|------|------|

### SECTION AND PART

| TOP | RIGHT | LEFT | BACK |
|-----|-------|------|------|

### APPLY

☐          ☐          ☐          ☐          ☐

**Instructor Signature** _____          **Date** _____

# 3-STRAND UNDERBRAID

View the video, complete the Design Decisions chart, then perform this workshop. Complete the self-check as you progress through the workshop.

**20 mins**
Suggested Salon Speed

| PREPARATION | ✔ |
|---|---|
| » Assemble tools and products<br>» Set up workstation | ☐ |

| HAIR PREPARATION – LONG SOLID LENGTHS | |
|---|---|
| » Blow dry hair straight, away from face<br>» Apply appropriate products<br>» Use paddle or large round brush | ☐ |

| DISTRIBUTE/SECTION/PART/APPLY | |
|---|---|
| 1. **Begin 3-strand underbraid with crescent-shaped section:**<br>» Distribute lengths straight back<br>» Take crescent-shaped section at front hairline<br>» Divide crescent-shaped section into 3 equal strands<br>» Cross right strand under center strand | ☐ |
| 2. **Cross left strand under center strand:**<br>» Complete 3-strand sequence<br><br>**Note:** It is acceptable to cross the right or the left strand under the center first, as long as you are consistent throughout. | ☐ |

3.  **Take diagonal parting on right side and join section to center strand.**

4.  **Repeat on left side:**
    - » Switch hands
    - » Always hold strands that you last crossed in one hand

5.  **Work from side to side using same technique:**
    - » Pick up consistent partings
    - » Maintain tension and control

6.  **Maintain tension working along curve of head:**
    - » Tilt head forward slightly
    - » Conform your hands to curve of head

7. **Work off-scalp:**
   >> Continue crossing right under center and left under center
   >> Work toward ends
   >> Secure with elastic band

8. **The finish shows an underbraid, which results in a projected braid appearance.**

**COMPLETION**

>> Discard single-use supplies
>> Disinfect tools and multi-use supplies
>> Disinfect workstation and arrange in proper order

**20 mins**
Suggested Salon Speed

**My Speed**
_____
_____
_____

**INSTRUCTIONS:**
Record your time in comparison with the suggested salon speed. Then, list here how you could improve your performance.

_____

_____

_____

_____

_____

# ON-THE-SCALP 3-STRAND BRAIDS

## EXPLORE

**Have you ever seen an intricate-looking on-the-scalp braided style and wondered how it was created?**

## INSPIRE

Once you master 3-strand on-the-scalp braids, you can create beautiful designs—from practical to high fashion, even avant-garde.

## ACHIEVE

Following this *On-the-Scalp 3-Strand Braids Workshop*, you'll be able to:

&raquo; Identify the long hair procedures related to on-the-scalp braids

&raquo; Create an on-the-scalp braid design with even tension and consistent partings throughout

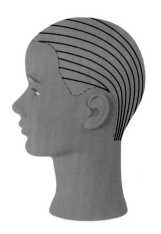

The finish shows an asymmetrical on-the-scalp braid design adapted to the contours of the head with hanging lengths at the nape.

The head is sectioned with a diagonal part from over the right eye to left of the apex and to the center nape. Partings on the heavier side follow the sectioning line. Modified diagonal partings are used on the lighter side. All partings narrow in the nape.

# LONG HAIR DESIGN PROCEDURES

1. DISTRIBUTE

2. SECTION

3. PART

4. APPLY

5. DETAIL

# ON-THE-SCALP 3-STRAND BRAIDS

Draw or fill in the boxes with the appropriate answers.

---

**DESIGN DECISIONS**

### OVERALL SHAPE, POSITION OF VOLUME AND DIRECTION OF DESIGN

| FRONT | RIGHT | LEFT | BACK |
|-------|-------|------|------|

---

### PREPARE

☐ BLOW DRY STRAIGHT     ☐ FLAT IRON

☐ BLOW DRY ROUND BRUSH     ☐ CURLING IRON

☐ THERMAL ROLLERS

PRODUCTS/SUPPLIES

_____

_____

_____

---

### DISTRIBUTE

| TOP | RIGHT | LEFT | BACK |
|-----|-------|------|------|

---

### SECTION AND PART

| TOP | RIGHT | LEFT | BACK |
|-----|-------|------|------|

---

### APPLY

☐     ☐     ☐     ☐     ☐

---

**Instructor Signature** _____ **Date** _____

# ON-THE-SCALP 3-STRAND BRAIDS

View the video, complete the Design Decisions chart, then perform this workshop. Complete the self-check as you progress through the workshop.

1 hr
30 mins
Suggested
Salon Speed

| PREPARATION | | ✔ |
|---|---|---|
| | >> Assemble tools and products <br> >> Set up workstation | ☐ |

### HAIR PREPARATION — INCREASE-LAYERED LENGTHS

| | | |
|---|---|---|
| | >> Air form hair straight, away from face <br> >> Flat iron if needed | ☐ |

### DISTRIBUTE/SECTION

| | | |
|---|---|---|
| | 1. **Section hair:** <br> >> Distribute lengths straight back <br> >> Diagonal part from over right eye to slightly left of apex <br><br> >> Apex to center nape | ☐ |

### PART/APPLY

| | | |
|---|---|---|
| | 2. **Release parting parallel to sectioning line from front hairline to nape.** | ☐ |

3. **Begin 3-strand on-the-scalp underbraid:**

   » Palm-down hand position
   » Pick up and cross outside strands under center strand using index finger and thumb
   » Use firm, even tension
   » Tilt head forward when working in nape

4. **Work off-scalp:**

   » When hairline is reached, work to ends

5. **Work toward left side using same partings and braiding technique:**

   » Maintain hand position
   » Use firm, even tension
   » Stay close to scalp working over curves of head

6. **Make partings and braids narrower as you reach nape area:**

   » Head may be tilted forward for comfort and ease

7. **Adapt partings on the side to follow contours of head.**

8. **Adapt partings to conform to hairline.**

   **Note:** Braids near the ear will not extend to the back.

9. **On right side, release and braid parting following hairline:**
   >> Start at temple area, extend to back of ear
   >> Braid off-scalp behind ear

10. **Work up hairline using same braiding technique:**
    >> Adapt subsequent partings to contours of head

11. **Take diagonal partings from sectioning line:**
    >> Curve to conform to previous partings
    >> Become vertical in back

12. **Work through to crown using curved partings:**
    >> Maintain even tension
    >> Braid off scalp to complete each braid
    >> Adjust partings as you work

## DETAIL  ✔

13. Trim ends if necessary.  ☐

14. Flat iron to create slight underbevel to complete design.  ☐

15. The finish shows a beautiful yet functional braided design that creates textural interest.  ☐

## COMPLETION

>> Discard single-use supplies
>> Disinfect tools and multi-use supplies
>> Disinfect workstation and arrange in proper order  ☐

**1 hr 30 mins**
Suggested Salon Speed

**My Speed**
_____
_____
_____

### INSTRUCTIONS:

Record your time in comparison with the suggested salon speed. Then, list here how you could improve your performance.

_____
_____
_____
_____
_____

### VARIATION — ON-THE-SCALP 3-STRAND BRAIDS

**A variation of on-the-scalp 3-strand braids is available online. This variation is performed on a live, male model and features alternating directions and curved lines, creating a graphic pattern.**

## SINGLE-STRAND
## COILED TWISTS

### EXPLORE

**How do you think a client transitioning from relaxed to natural hair could benefit from this design?**

### INSPIRE

Knowing how to perform the frequently requested single-strand, coiled twists design, which offers two finished-look options, can be quite lucrative.

### ACHIEVE

Following this *Single-Strand, Coiled Twists Workshop*, you'll be able to:

>> Identify the long hair procedures as related to the single-strand, coiled twists design

>> Create knots by twisting, coiling and wrapping strands around themselves

>> Create springy, curled texture by loosening coiled twists

Single-strand, coiled twists, commonly known as "Bantu knots," create a modern, in-demand look while set. When the knots are opened and loosened, the result is a wavy, curly style, depending on hair length.

Triangular bases are used throughout. Coiled, twisted knots are positioned at the center of their bases.

# LONG HAIR DESIGN PROCEDURES

1. DISTRIBUTE

2. SECTION

3. PART

4. APPLY

5. DETAIL

# SINGLE-STRAND COILED TWISTS

Draw or fill in the boxes with the appropriate answers.

## DESIGN DECISIONS

### OVERALL SHAPE, POSITION OF VOLUME AND DIRECTION OF DESIGN

| FRONT | RIGHT | LEFT | BACK |
|---|---|---|---|

### PREPARE

☐ BLOW DRY STRAIGHT    ☐ FLAT IRON

_____% - _____%    ☐ CURLING IRON

☐ BLOW DRY ROUND BRUSH    ☐ THERMAL ROLLERS

PRODUCTS/SUPPLIES

_____

_____

_____

### PROJECT

| FRONT | RIGHT | LEFT | BACK |
|---|---|---|---|

### SECTION AND PART

| TOP | RIGHT | LEFT | BACK |
|---|---|---|---|

### APPLY

☐     ☐     ☐     ☐     ☐

**Instructor Signature** _____ **Date** _____

PERFORMANCE GUIDE
# SINGLE-STRAND COILED TWISTS

View the video, complete the Design Decisions chart, then perform this workshop. Complete the self-check as you progress through the workshop.

**1 hr 30 mins**
Suggested Salon Speed

| **PREPARATION** | ✔ |
|---|---|
| >> Assemble tools and products<br>>> Set up workstation<br>>> Shampoo and condition uniformly layered, tightly curled hair | ☐ |

### HAIR PREPARATION

**1. Detangle and protect freshly shampooed hair:**
>> Use wide-tooth comb
>> Work from ends to base
>> Work from nape to top of head
>> Center to either side

☐

**2. Apply thermal protectant throughout head:**
>> Work through hair using fingers to part and apply product
>> Reapply as necessary
>> Work from nape to top
>> Distribute with comb

☐

**3. Section hair into 5 sections:**
>> Behind apex to back of each ear
>> Center of each eye back to sectioning line
>> Apex to center nape

☐

**4. Reduce curl pattern by approximately 75%-85%:**
>> Release 1"-1½" (2.5-3.75 cm) horizontal parting across both sections at nape
>> Stretch hair with tension using 9-row brush
>> Direct airflow from base to ends
>> Air form from base to midstrand, then midstrand to ends
>> Work from center to either side; bottom to top
>> Air form side sections from bottom to top
>> Air form top section from back to front hairline

☐

5. **Resection then section and apply coiled twists in lower nape:**
   >> Tilt head slightly forward
   >> Part horizontally across nape from middle of each ear
   >> Part diagonally from center of sectioning line to corners of nape hairline to create 3 triangular sections
   >> At center, apply and distribute setting product through strand; apply light gel to ends if necessary
   >> Converge and project strand at 90° from center of base
   >> Twist in clockwise direction (right) with firm, even tension and hand-over-hand technique

6. **Twist approximately ¾ of the length; wrap strand around base in same direction:**
   >> Keep fingers close to base; twist to ends
   >> Tuck and secure ends using tail comb

7. **Repeat same twist technique to complete this section:**
   >> Twist right strand in clockwise direction (right)
   >> Twist left strand in counterclockwise direction (left)

8. **Section and apply coiled twists in next section:**
   >> Release horizontal section at top of ear
   >> At center, part diagonally; create triangular base with narrow end at bottom
   >> Subsection and clip alternating triangles of similar size
   >> Twist and coil center strand in clockwise direction
   >> Tuck and wrap to secure ends

9. **Continue to use same parting and twisting technique to complete this section:**
   >> Twist strands toward right side clockwise
   >> Twist strands toward left side counterclockwise

**CREST**                                                                                                   ✓

10. **Section and apply coiled twists through crest area:**
    >> Section horizontally along crest, including sides
    >> Create center triangle with wide end at bottom
    >> Part diagonally to create a triangular base
    >> Subsection and clip alternating triangles
    >> Twist and coil center and right subsections clockwise
    >> Twist and coil left subsections counterclockwise

□

**UPPER CROWN**

11. **Section upper crown within a horseshoe-shaped section:**
    >> Section horizontally from center of each eye to upper crown
    >> Alternate position of center triangle
    >> Subsection alternating triangles

□

12. **Apply coiled twists in horseshoe-shaped section:**
    >> Twist and coil center and right subsections clockwise
    >> Twist and coil left subsections counterclockwise

□

**TOP**

13. **Section horizontally in front of and behind apex, creating 3 sections:**
    >> Use pivotal partings to create 3 triangular bases in crown

□

14. **Twist and coil center and right triangles clockwise and left triangle in counterclockwise direction.**

□

15. Within the apex section, use crisscross diagonal partings to create 4 triangular bases.

16. **Twist and coil each triangular base:**
    >> Twist front and back sections in clockwise direction
    >> Twist right section clockwise
    >> Twist left section counterclockwise

17. **Subsection front section in same manner:**
    >> Twist front and back sections in clockwise direction
    >> Twist right section clockwise
    >> Twist left section counterclockwise

18. **This finish shows coiled twists throughout positioned within triangular bases:**
    >> Allow hair to dry under hood dryer

**LOOSEN AND DETAIL**

19. **Perform strand test at crown, nape and front hairline to confirm hair is dry:**
    >> Unwind opposite twisted direction; split each strand in half at base
    >> Feel along strand for moisture and visually check for frizz
    >> If moisture or frizz is present, re-twist and allow more drying time

**20. Loosen twists throughout head:**

>> Starting at nape, unwrap each twist in opposite direction and split strand in half at base
>> Continue splitting smaller strands
>> Twist smaller strands in initial direction then release

**21. Continue to loosen and separate each triangle, working toward top:**

>> Work from one side to other within each row

**22. Lift hair at base using a wide-tooth comb or pick to blend bases if necessary:**

>> Apply appropriate finishing product for hold and shine

**23. The loosened finish shows highly activated, and slightly irregular curled texture. This texture is more defined than the natural texture, yet not as uniform as a set on rollers or rods.**

**COMPLETION**

>> Discard single-use supplies
>> Disinfect tools and multi-use supplies
>> Disinfect workstation and arrange in proper order

**1 hr 30 mins**
Suggested Salon Speed

**My Speed**
_____
_____
_____

**INSTRUCTIONS:**

Record your time in comparison with the suggested salon speed. Then, list here how you could improve your performance.

_____
_____
_____
_____
_____

## 5-STRAND LOOPS

### EXPLORE

**Can you describe a variety of designs, incorporating direction and movement, that can be created with loops?**

### INSPIRE

Loop designs are a favorite of many bridal clients. Knowing how to alter the position and height of loops to complement facial features will prove to be quite lucrative.

### ACHIEVE

Following this *5-Strand Loops Workshop*, you'll be able to:

>> Identify the long hair procedures related to the 5-strand loop design

>> Create a well-balanced long hair design that incorporates 5-strand loops from a ponytail positioned at the upper crown

The finish shows a beautiful
5-strand loop design positioned
in the upper crown.

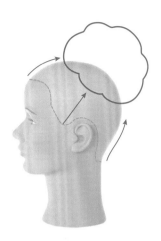

Distribution is away from the face
and volume is positioned at the
upper crown.

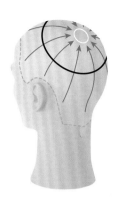

The hair is distributed toward the
upper crown to position
the ponytail.

# LONG HAIR DESIGN PROCEDURES

1. DISTRIBUTE

2. SECTION

3. PART          N/A

4. APPLY

5. DETAIL

# 5-STRAND LOOPS

Draw or fill in the boxes with the appropriate answers.

## DESIGN DECISIONS

### OVERALL SHAPE, POSITION OF VOLUME AND DIRECTION OF DESIGN

| FRONT | RIGHT | LEFT | BACK |
|---|---|---|---|

### PREPARATION

PRODUCTS/SUPPLIES

- ☐ BLOW DRY STRAIGHT
- ☐ BLOW DRY ROUND BRUSH
- ☐ FLAT IRON
- ☐ CURLING IRON
- ☐ THERMAL ROLLERS

_____

_____

_____

### DISTRIBUTE

| TOP | RIGHT | LEFT | BACK |
|---|---|---|---|

### SECTION AND PART

| TOP | RIGHT | LEFT | BACK |
|---|---|---|---|

### APPLY

| ☐ | ☐ | ☐ | ☐ | ☐ |
|---|---|---|---|---|

**Instructor Signature** _____     **Date** _____

PERFORMANCE GUIDE

# 5-STRAND LOOPS

View the video, complete the Design Decisions chart, then perform this workshop. Complete the self-check as you progress through the workshop.

**30 mins**
Suggested
Salon Speed

| PREPARATION | | ✔ |
|---|---|---|
| | » Assemble tools and products<br>» Set up workstation | ☐ |

**HAIR PREPARATION – LONG SOLID LENGTHS**

| | » Air form hair straight, away from face, toward position of ponytail | ☐ |
|---|---|---|

**DISTRIBUTE/SECTION/APPLY**

| | 1. **Distribute and section hair:**<br>» Distribute hair from front hairline, sides and perimeter toward upper crown<br>» Position ponytail<br>» Subdivide ponytail into 5 equal strands<br>   ▪ 5th strand at center of ponytail<br>» Secure with clips | ☐ |
|---|---|---|
| | 2. **Backcomb underneath 1st strand for support:**<br>» Use fine-tooth tail comb | ☐ |

3. **Smooth top surface of strand:**

&gt;&gt; Hairspray for control

4. **Use index and middle fingers to fold strand toward right and direct ends toward left.**

   **Note:** The position of your fingers along the strand determines the size of the loop.

5. **Position loop diagonally and secure with bobby pins:**

&gt;&gt; Wrap remaining ends around your finger and tuck inside loop
&gt;&gt; Secure ends with bobby pins

6. **Expand loop and close one end:**

&gt;&gt; Hairspray for control

   **Note:** You may use long hairpins to control the shape while working.

7. **Use same technique to create next (2nd) loop:**
   - Backcomb and smooth strand
   - Fold and position loop diagonally
   - Secure with bobby pins
   - Tuck ends inside loop and secure
   - Expand shape and close one end

8. **Repeat same technique with 3rd loop.**

9. **Fold 4th loop to right and position diagonally:**
   - Repeat same techniques

10. **Secure base of 5th strand to first loop:**
    - Directing strand toward left
    - Secure with bobby pin

**11. Position and secure 5th loop:**

>> Direct strand toward right
>> Secure at center using bobby pins or hairpins
>> On top of other four loops
>> Tuck ends and close loop at back
>> Check form for balance

**12. The length of the hair will also influence the size of the loops for this design. Strive to create consistent loops within the design.**

**COMPLETION**

>> Discard single-use supplies
>> Disinfect tools and multi-use supplies
>> Disinfect workstation and arrange in proper order

**30 mins**
Suggested
Salon Speed

My Speed
_____
_____
_____

**INSTRUCTIONS:**

Record your time in comparison with the suggested salon speed. Then, list here how you could improve your performance.

_____

_____

_____

_____

_____

## VERTICAL ROLL

### EXPLORE

**How many ways do you think rolls can be used in conjunction with other long hair techniques?**

### INSPIRE

The smooth, unbroken texture of the vertical roll is what gives it timeless appeal. Mastering vertical rolls will allow you to create a multitude of looks—from elegant and classic to cutting-edge contemporary.

### ACHIEVE

Following this *Vertical Roll Workshop*, you'll be able to:

» Identify the long hair procedures related to the vertical roll design

» Create a well-balanced long hair design that creates an elongated shape with smooth texture throughout

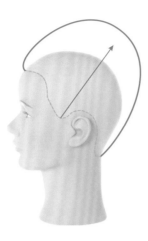

Sometimes referred to as a French twist, the finish shows an elongated look that can be adapted to medium lengths and a variety of textures.

To create this elongated shape, the hair is distributed diagonally away from the face and volume is positioned predominantly at the crown.

Hair on the left side is distributed toward the right and pinned slightly off-center. Diagonal partings are used to subdivide the sections on the right side.

# LONG HAIR DESIGN PROCEDURES

1. DISTRIBUTE

2. SECTION

3. PART

4. APPLY

5. DETAIL

# VERTICAL ROLL

Draw or fill in the boxes with the appropriate answers.

---

**DESIGN DECISIONS**

**OVERALL SHAPE, POSITION OF VOLUME AND DIRECTION OF DESIGN**

| FRONT | RIGHT | LEFT | BACK |

---

**PREPARATION**

☐ BLOW DRY STRAIGHT     ☐ FLAT IRON

☐ BLOW DRY ROUND BRUSH     ☐ CURLING IRON

☐ THERMAL ROLLERS

PRODUCTS/SUPPLIES

_____

_____

_____

---

**DISTRIBUTE**

| TOP | RIGHT | LEFT | BACK |

---

**SECTION AND PART**

| TOP | RIGHT | LEFT | BACK |

---

**APPLY**

☐     ☐     ☐     ☐     ☐

---

**Instructor Signature** _____ **Date** _____

# VERTICAL ROLL

View the video, complete the Design Decisions chart, then perform
this workshop. Complete the self-check as you progress through
the workshop.

**30 mins**
Suggested
Salon Speed

| **PREPARATION** | | ✔ |
|---|---|---|
| | » Assemble tools and products <br> » Set up workstation | ☐ |

## HAIR PREPARATION — LONG INCREASE-LAYERED LENGTHS

| | | |
|---|---|---|
| | » Set hair lengths on thermal rollers | ☐ |

## SECTION/DISTRIBUTE/PART/APPLY

| | | |
|---|---|---|
| | **1. Section at front hairline using crescent-shaped parting:** <br> » To be worked into last part of roll | ☐ |
| | **2. Isolate small, slightly off-center triangle at base of nape.** | ☐ |

3. Distribute hair from left side over to right side.

4. Interlock slightly off-center row of bobby pins vertically:
   >> Establishes position of roll
   >> Position pins with open end facing upward
   >> Secure last bobby pin in downward direction

5. Backcomb base of triangle section, smooth surface upward and fold section over bobby pins:
   >> Use right hand to fold section over bobby pins while using left hand to control ends

6. Secure inside of roll with bobby pins or hairpins.

7. **Wrap remaining lengths around finger and pin just in front of roll:**
   - Acts as filler for next section

8. **Take next diagonal parting, distribute lengths upward and fold section over filler.**

9. **Secure inside of roll and create filler for next section:**
   - Blend each section into previous one to avoid splits
   - Secure inside of roll with bobby pins

10. **Continue to use same techniques as you work to the top:**
    - Note that size of roll increases

11. **At top of roll, shift slightly to the left:**
    - Helps balance form when viewed from front

✔

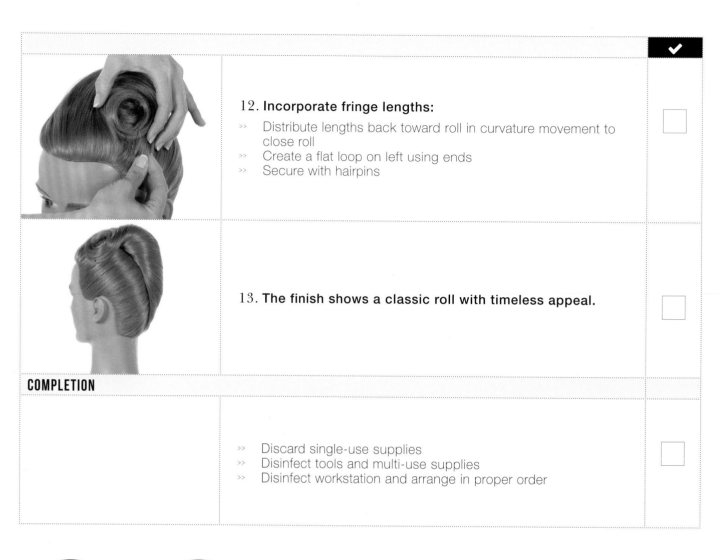

**12.** **Incorporate fringe lengths:**

>> Distribute lengths back toward roll in curvature movement to close roll
>> Create a flat loop on left using ends
>> Secure with hairpins

**13.** **The finish shows a classic roll with timeless appeal.**

### COMPLETION

>> Discard single-use supplies
>> Disinfect tools and multi-use supplies
>> Disinfect workstation and arrange in proper order

**30 mins**
Suggested
Salon Speed

My Speed
_____
_____
_____

### INSTRUCTIONS:

Record your time in comparison with the suggested salon speed. Then, list here how you could improve your performance.

_____
_____
_____
_____

### VARIATION — VERTICAL ROLL — SOLID FORM

**A variation on the vertical roll using the end of a large tail comb is available online. This variation requires less pinning and is recommended for extra long, solid lengths.**